"Warm, engaging, and infinitely valuable, Dr. Harris has written the ideal book for couples who are seeking to strengthen their relationships and grow intimacy. Harris's *ACT with Love* takes acceptance and commitment therapy into the realm of couplehood in a kind, thoughtful, and realistic way. Share it with couples everywhere and use it in your own relationship. I plan to!"

—Robyn D. Walser, Ph.D., author of *The Mindful Couple*

"Not since *Masters and Johnson on Sex and Human Loving* has there been such a powerful, practical, and inspiring book written about love and relationships. Russ Harris really is a genius with words as well as an expert ACT clinician. With these qualities he succeeds in weaving together a path to successful relationships. Don't miss this book!"

—JoAnne Dahl, Ph.D., associate psychology professor at the University of Uppsala in Sweden

"Reading and following this book may well be the most precious gift you ever give not only to your partner, but also to yourself. I highly recommended it to those who wish to revitalize a floundering relationship as well as those who want to make a good relationship even better."

—Robert D. Zettle, Ph.D., associate psychology professor at Wichita State University and author of *ACT for Depression*

"If you want to be the best mate you can be in your relationship, this book will help. If both you and your mate want to have the best relationship you can have, this book will help that, too!"

—Hank Robb, Ph.D., ABPP

ACT *with love*

stop struggling, reconcile differences, and strengthen your relationship with acceptance and commitment therapy

RUSS HARRIS, MD

New Harbinger Publications, Inc.

Publisher's Note

Distributed in Canada by Raincoast Books

Copyright © 2009 by Russ Harris
            New Harbinger Publications, Inc.
            5674 Shattuck Avenue
            Oakland, CA 94609
            www.newharbinger.com

Cover design by Amy Shoup
Text design by Amy Shoup and Michele Waters-Kermes
Acquired by Tesilya Hanauer
Edited by Jean Blomquist

Library of Congress Cataloging in Publication Data on file

Printed in the United States of America

18   17   16

20   19   18   17   16   15   14   13

contents

series editor letter   v

acknowledgments   vii

introduction: it's a messy business   1

PART 1
making a mess

CHAPTER 1   mission impossible?   9

CHAPTER 2   what's your problem?   16

PART 2
making a commitment

CHAPTER 3   should I stay or should I go?   27

CHAPTER 4   does it take two to tango?   33

PART 3
making it work

CHAPTER 5   you're both hurting   43

CHAPTER 6   everyone's a control freak!   54

CHAPTER 7	look inside your heart	61
CHAPTER 8	into the smog	75
CHAPTER 9	the judgment machine	88
CHAPTER 10	gripping stories	98
CHAPTER 11	the kiss of life	105
CHAPTER 12	name it and tame it	111
CHAPTER 13	look at me! look at me!	122
CHAPTER 14	the heart of the battle	129
CHAPTER 15	take off the armor	137
CHAPTER 16	the power of asking nicely	147
CHAPTER 17	you can't always get what you want	155
CHAPTER 18	open your eyes	163
CHAPTER 19	sticky situations	176
CHAPTER 20	the christmas truce	184
CHAPTER 21	intimacy	189
CHAPTER 22	old word, new take	198
CHAPTER 23	building a trust fund	202
CHAPTER 24	let your self go	207
CHAPTER 25	and now, time for some fun!	212
CHAPTER 26	the adventure continues	216
	appendix: when it's over, it's over	223
	resources	225
	recommended reading	226
	references	227

Dear Reader:

Welcome to New Harbinger Publications. New Harbinger is dedicated to publishing books based on acceptance and commitment therapy (ACT) and its application to specific areas. New Harbinger has a long-standing reputation as a publisher of quality, well-researched books for general and professional audiences.

ACT *with Love* is perhaps the best book on love and relationships that we have come across in our professional careers. That's because this book is about acting with love in *any* close personal relationship, including the relationship you have with yourself. This book will help you avoid repeating the mistakes of the past and falling back into patterns of behavior that have not worked for you. It is a beautiful, uplifting book that will benefit you whether you are currently in a good or bad partner relationship, or in no relationship at all. Although the book is written for anyone interested in improving partner relationships or getting back into one, it will also help you improve your relationship with the person you are closest to in the most basic and natural way: yourself.

This book goes beyond the scope of most of the numerous books on love and relationships. Those books typically focus on aspects of relationships that may be in need of improvement by providing well-meaning advice and occasionally some skills. In contrast to books that get bogged down with analyzing relationship patterns, family dynamics, or other complex systems, this book is disarmingly simple (but not at all simplistic) and free of psychological jargon. It gives realistic hope without promising too much or raising false expectations. Like many books in the Acceptance and Commitment Therapy Series, this book does not just provide explanations, insights, and advice. It offers you plenty of opportunities to learn—in very concrete ways—how to have more open, honest, and fulfilling relationships by innovatively and creatively applying ACT principles to relationships. In just about every chapter, Russ Harris invites you to do a variety of engaging, practical experiential exercises that will bring the material alive and make it personally meaningful to you. The chapter titles are as intriguing and thoughtful as the text that follows. The most important themes are revisited throughout the book so you can consolidate your progress.

Although the book is well grounded in the empirical research base of ACT, it speaks to you from the author's heart as well as his brain.

That is why it can touch you in a profound way—if you stay open to its messages. You can work through the book on your own or with a partner. Some of the exercises are designed to be done with a partner. However, having a (willing) partner is not a prerequisite for benefiting from this book. You can learn the skills by yourself and for yourself. What you learn from this book will enlighten and enrich your life no matter what your current relationship situation is.

As part of New Harbinger's commitment to publishing books based on sound, scientific, clinical research, we oversee all prospective books for the Acceptance and Commitment Therapy Series. Serving as series editors, we comment on proposals and offer guidance as needed, and use a gentle hand in making suggestions regarding the content, depth, and scope of each book.

Books in the Acceptance and Commitment Therapy Series:

- Have an adequate database, appropriate to the strength of the claims being made.

- Are theoretically coherent. They will fit with the ACT model and underlying behavioral principles as they have evolved at the time of writing.

- Do not overlap needlessly with existing volumes.

- Avoid jargon and unnecessary entanglement with proprietary methods, leaving ACT work open and available.

- Keep the focus always on what is good for the reader.

- Support the further development of the field.

Provide information in a way that is of practical use to readers.

These guidelines reflect the values of the broader ACT community. You'll see all of them packed into this book. This series is meant to offer information that can truly be helpful in alleviating human suffering. This book certainly fulfills that mission.

Sincerely,

Georg H. Eifert, Ph.D.,
John Forsyth, Ph.D.,
and Steven C. Hayes, Ph.D.

acknowledgments

Behind every book, there's a cast of thousands. Here I'd like to give special thanks to a few of those "cast members." My first thanks—and my last as well, as you'll see shortly—go to my wife, Carmel, for all her love and support. She has not only graciously tolerated my total absorption on the computer for hours on end and my extensive absences from home to run interstate workshops, but she has also given me all sorts of useful input and patiently helped me to develop and clarify my ideas.

Thanks also to all those friends, relatives, and colleagues who read early drafts and gave me invaluable feedback: Margaret Denman, Louise Hayes, Joe Parsons, Genghis Lloyd-Harris, Kim Paleg, and Joanne Steinwachs.

Words can't really express the enormous gratitude I feel toward Steve Hayes, the originator of ACT. Let's face it: without ACT, this book (and my career) would not exist. That gratitude naturally extends to Kelly Wilson, Kirk Strosahl, John Forsyth, Hank Robb, and the entire ACT community. I feel very fortunate to belong to such a community, not only because it is so supportive but also because so many of the ideas in this book have arisen from the open discussions within it. Of course I've also been positively influenced by many people outside of ACT, most notably by the couples work of John Gottman and the rational emotive behavior therapy of Albert Ellis—so thanks, John and Al!

I'd also like to thank my agent, Sammie Justesen, for her continuing support and advice. Plus a heap of thanks to the entire team at New Harbinger—including Jess Beebe, Tesilya Hanauer, and Matt McKay—not only for their faith in this book but also for all the "hard yakka" they've put into it. And extra-special thanks to editor Jean Blomquist for her great work in trimming the fat from this book and knocking it into shape.

Last but not least, I want to thank the two people who have most helped me to learn, and grow, and experience what true love is: my wife, Carmel, and my son, Max.

introduction:
it's a messy business

Relationships are both wonderful and terrible. They can give us the highest of highs and the lowest of lows, send us soaring into the stratosphere on wings of love, or drop us from on high to splat in the mud. In those early days of your relationship, when you're holding your partner tenderly in your arms, and your heart's pounding against your rib cage like a professional boxer, it's hard to believe that one day, in the not-too-distant future, all those blissful feelings will be gone. That's right—gone. Disappeared. Vanished without a trace. And in their place might be anger, fear, sorrow, frustration, loneliness, regret, or despair, or perhaps even bitterness, contempt, disgust, or hatred.

Why should this be so? Well, the simple fact is this: feelings change. They are like the weather. Even during the hottest summer or the coldest winter, the weather continually changes—and our emotions are no different. So no matter how wonderful your partner, no matter how great your relationship, those initial feelings of love will not last. But don't be alarmed. Although they will inevitably disappear, they will also come back again. And then they will go again. And then they'll come back again. And so on, and so on, and so on, until the day you die. And it's the same deal with every human emotion—from fear and anger to joy and bliss. Feelings come and they go, surely as spring follows winter.

Most of us know this at some level, but we easily forget it. We get hooked on those loving feelings and expect them to last. We expect our partners to meet our needs, behave the way we want them to, fulfill our wishes, and generally make our lives better, easier, and happier—and then we get upset when reality clashes with our fantasy. The great joke about being human is that the people we spend the most time with and know most intimately are the very same people who "push our buttons" the most. And while a snide remark, cold rejection, harsh criticism, or angry outburst may be unpleasant coming from our boss, a neighbor, or a coworker, it hurts far more when it comes from the person we love. There is no getting away from this: love makes us vulnerable. If we allow ourselves to be intimate and open with another—to let that person past our defenses and into our heart—then we allow ourselves to get hurt. Love and pain are like intimate dance partners—they go hand in hand. Don't take my word for this—check out your own experience: have you ever had a close relationship with anybody and spent significant amounts of time in his or her company without experiencing some sort of painful feelings as a result of your interaction?

So basically it's like this: if you own a house, you're guaranteed to have maintenance costs and fuel bills; if you have a baby, you're guaranteed to have dirty diapers and sleepless nights; and if you build an intimate relationship, you're guaranteed to have a certain amount of pain and stress. This is one of the inconvenient truths of being human. Sharing your life with another human being can be an amazing, uplifting, awe-inspiring experience—and at other times, it can be absolutely dreadful. Pop stars, poets, romance novelists, and greeting-card companies have a vested interest in ignoring this inconvenient truth. They want you to believe all those ancient myths: that there really is a perfect partner out there just waiting for you; that without this person, you are incomplete, unfulfilled, and doomed to a life half-lived; that when you do eventually find this perfect partner, you will fall in love and remain in that blissful state effortlessly and forever.

Of course, I'm being flippant here. But the fact is, almost all of us walk around with a lot of unrealistic expectations about love, relationships, and intimacy—beliefs continually reinforced throughout our lives by movies, novels, plays, songs, TV, poetry, magazines, newspapers, office gossip, well-meaning friends, and even self-help books. Unfortunately if we let these misleading ideas guide our lives and try to base our relationships on them, then we will find ourselves in a vicious cycle whereby our very attempts to create lasting love will ultimately destroy it.

Our misguided attempts to find love are wreaking havoc in modern society. In most Western countries, the divorce rate is now close to 50 percent—and of those marriages that last, many are full of emptiness, loneliness, and misery. Increasingly people are afraid to commit to a long-term relationship (married or not), terrified that it will all end in tears, bitterness, or lawsuits. No wonder there are now more single adults living alone than ever before in history.

Does this all sound a bit grim, gloomy, and depressing? Fear not. The good news is, there is a way to bring some order to this messy business—and this book will show you exactly how to do it. Within these pages, you'll discover how to let go of unhelpful beliefs and attitudes about love; how to realistically create an authentic, intimate, loving long-term relationship; and how to deal with the painful thoughts and feelings that all such relationships inevitably cause. You'll learn how to handle sadness, rejection, and fear; how to deal effectively with anger, frustration, and resentment; how to forgive both yourself and your partner; and how to rebuild trust if it has been shattered. You'll learn how to reduce the amount of tension and stress associated with negotiating your needs and reconciling your differences—and how to turn the pain and hurt of conflict into caring and compassion.

acceptance and commitment therapy for relationships

This book is based on a revolutionary new development in human psychology: an approach known as acceptance and commitment therapy, or ACT. ACT (which should be pronounced as the word "act," not as the letters A-C-T) was created in the United States by psychologist Steven Hayes and further developed by a number of his colleagues, including Kirk Strosahl and Kelly Wilson (Hayes, Strosahl, and Wilson 1999). ACT is a scientifically based therapy that has proven effective with a vast range of painful human conditions—from depression and drug addiction to work stress and schizophrenia. Intriguingly, although ACT is based on cutting-edge research in behavioral psychology, it has striking parallels with many ancient Eastern traditions.

ACT is based on a set of powerful principles that together enable you to develop "psychological flexibility." Scientific research is increasingly revealing that the higher our level of psychological flexibility, the greater our quality of life. So what does the term actually mean? Well, *psychological flexibility* is the ability to adapt to a situation with openness, awareness, and focus, and to take effective action guided by your values (your heart's deepest desires for who you want to be and what you want to stand for in life). Sound confusing? Let me break it down.

There are two key components to psychological flexibility:

1. The ability to be psychologically present: a mental state commonly known as "mindfulness." Mindfulness enables you

   ■ to be fully aware of your here-and-now experience, with an attitude of openness and curiosity;

   ■ to be engaged and absorbed in what you are doing;

   ■ to reduce the influence and impact of painful thoughts and feelings.

2. The ability to take effective action. In other words, to take action that is

   ■ conscious and deliberate, rather than impulsive or mindless;

   ■ motivated, guided, and inspired by your core values;

   ■ flexible and adaptable to the demands of the situation.

Put more simply, psychological flexibility is the ability to be present, open up, and do what matters. As you increase your psychological flexibility, you will be more able to effectively handle difficult feelings, disrupt unhelpful thought processes, rise above self-limiting beliefs, focus on and engage in what you are doing, and change ineffective or self-defeating behaviors so you can build better relationships.

Although ACT was originally developed for problems such as depression and anxiety, its core principles can readily be applied to relationship issues with great effect. As you progress through this book, one major emphasis will be on the development of mindfulness—your ability to be fully aware, with an attitude of openness and curiosity. Another major emphasis will be on clarifying your values—your heart's deepest desires for who you want to be and what you want to stand for in life—and using them to guide your actions. And although we'll be focusing on intimate relationships, such as with your spouse or partner, you can apply these principles to enhance and enrich any relationship that matters to you, whether it's with your children, parents, friends, neighbors, or fellow workers.

who is this book for?

This book is aimed at common relationship issues, the type that almost all couples will experience; it does not cover more extreme relationship issues such as domestic violence or severe addictions. I've written it for four different categories of reader:

- Your relationship is in reasonable shape, but you want to enrich it.

- Your relationship is in bad shape, but you want to repair it.

- You're not currently in a relationship, but you want to learn what went wrong in the last one so you're better prepared for the next one.

- You're a therapist, counselor, or coach looking for ideas on how to work with relationship issues.

If you're in either of the first two categories, then your partner may be willing to work through this book with you. However, one of the strengths of this book is that it allows you to unilaterally improve your relationship, even if your partner isn't interested.

how to use this book

ACT with Love is divided into three parts. In part 1, Making a Mess, we look at what goes wrong in relationships. In part 2, Making a Commitment, we look at whether you should stay or leave your relationship, and consider what is required if you truly want to stay and make it work. In part 3, Making It Work, we look at what sort of partner you want to be, what thoughts and feelings are getting in the way, and how mindfulness can help you to handle them much better. We also cover the inevitability of conflict and pain, and how you can reconcile your differences more effectively. And finally we look at ways to actively strengthen and deepen your relationship forevermore!

As you read, you will meet couples who have various relationship issues, some of which may be similar to yours. While I have worked with many people with relationship issues over the years, the stories of the people you will meet in this book are composites. I have changed their names and the details of their stories to thoroughly protect their confidentiality. Although these stories do not precisely match any real person's life, they certainly represent the struggles and successes of couples experiencing relationship issues.

Throughout the book, we will return again and again to a few basic principles of ACT, and you will learn how to apply them to make both yourself and your relationship thrive. Of course simply reading this book won't change anything. If you read a book on tennis, that alone won't make you a tennis player; you actually have to get out and hit some balls. Same deal with your relationship. If you want it to improve, you'll need to practice and apply what you read within these pages. And doing so can be hard work at times. There's no two ways about it: building a loving relationship—or repairing one that's in ruins—takes time, effort, and commitment. But of this I am very confident: if you consistently apply the approaches within this book, you will bring far more richness and love into your life. So if you think that's something worth investing in, then keep reading.

PART 1

Making a Mess

CHAPTER 1

mission impossible?

Falling in love is easy. Anyone can do it. It's like eating your favorite food or watching a great movie—lots of pleasure, no effort involved. But staying in love—now that's a real challenge, a challenge that's all the greater because of all the stuff and nonsense that's been pumped into our heads over the years. From our very first fairy tales, in which the prince and princess lived happily ever after, to the Hollywood endings of most popular movies, books, and TV shows, we hear and see the same old myths again and again. Here are the big four:

myth 1: the perfect partner

Did you know that somewhere out there, in the big wide world, there is a perfect match for you? Yes, it's true. The man or woman of your dreams is out there, hopelessly lost, just killing time, waiting for you to find him or her. Seek, and ye shall find a partner who will fulfill all your fantasies, meet all your needs, and live with you in everlasting bliss.

Yeah, right. And Santa Claus is real too.

Truth is, there's no such thing as the perfect partner, just as there's no such thing as the perfect couple. (As the old joke goes, there are only two types of couples: those who have a wonderful relationship, and those whom you know really well.) But how hard is it to truly let go of this idea? How hard is it to stop comparing your partner to others? To stop fantasizing about the partner you could have had, or would have had, or should have had? Or about the partner you really did have, but for one reason or another it didn't last? How hard is it to stop dwelling on your partner's faults and flaws and shortcomings, and thinking about how life would be so much better if only your partner would change?

Answer: very hard indeed, for most normal human beings. But it doesn't have to remain that way. Change is possible, if you want it. Let's just take a moment to look at what it is costing you to get all caught up in these patterns of thinking. How much frustration, anger, and disappointment does it create for you? Of course, I'm not advocating that you let your partner do as she pleases, whenever she wants, without any consideration for you; that would not give rise to a healthy, vital relationship. What I am advocating is that you take an honest look at your own internalized beliefs about how your partner *should* behave and what your relationship *should* be like; notice all the negative judgments you make about your partner and your relationship; and notice how these thoughts affect you when you get caught up in them. Are they helping your relationship or harming it?

myth 2: you complete me

When it comes to movies, I'm a big sucker for romantic comedies: *Four Weddings and a Funeral, Bridget Jones's Diary, When Harry Met Sally.* I just love them. One of my favorites was *Jerry Maguire*, which gave us the great phrase, "You complete me." This is the phrase that Jerry Maguire says to his girlfriend at the very end of the movie, to prove how much he loves her—at which point, I suddenly choked on my popcorn!

This is such an unhelpful idea to buy into. If you go along with this myth and act as if you are incomplete without your partner, then you set yourself up for all sorts of problems. You will be needy, dependent, and fearful of being alone, which is not conducive to a healthy, vital relationship. Fortunately what you'll discover as you keep reading is that you are already complete—regardless of whether you have a partner or not. Of course your mind will not readily agree to this—at least not if it's like the minds of most other people on this planet. Our minds are naturally self-critical, and they seem to revel in telling us how incomplete we all are. But despite what your mind may protest, as you work through this book, you will experience a sense of wholeness and completeness within yourself that is independent of anyone else. This will allow you to be more true to yourself in your relationship: to express yourself honestly, ask for what you need, and stand up for yourself without holding back for fear of rejection or abandonment.

myth 3: love should be easy

Love should be easy. Hmmmmm. Let's look at this proposition more closely.

When you live intimately for a long period of time with another human being who has (a) different thoughts and feelings, (b) different interests, (c) different expectations about housework, sex, money, religion, parenting, holidays, work-life balance, and quality time, (d) different styles for communicating, negotiating, and expressing himself, (e) different reactions to the things that you enjoy or fear or detest, (f) different drives for food, sex, sport, play, and work, (g) different standards of cleanliness and tidiness, (h) friends and relatives that you don't get on with too well, (i) lifelong, deeply entrenched habits and quirks that annoy you … it should be easy?

Does that sound convincing to you?

Of course, our minds are quick to point out that if our partners were more compatible, if they didn't have so many differences from us, then our relationships would be much easier. Good point, but now we're right back to myth 1: the perfect partner. The fact is there will always be significant differences between you and your partner in some or all the areas mentioned here and also in many others. That's why relationships *aren't* easy. They require communication, negotiation, compromise, and a lot of acceptance of differences; they also require you to stand up for yourself, to be honest about your desires and your feelings, and—in some situations, where something vitally important to your health and well-being is at stake—to absolutely refuse to compromise. This is quite a challenge. But as long as you expect your partner to think and feel and act like you, you're setting yourself up for disappointment and frustration.

Now there's no denying, some couples have more in common than others. Some couples are naturally optimistic, calm, and easygoing. Some couples have excellent communication skills. Some couples have very similar interests. And let's face it, if you're both passionately mad about rock climbing, it's a lot easier to agree on your vacation plans than if one of you loves sunbathing on the beach and the other absolutely hates it. But no matter how much you have in common, there will always be differences that challenge you. Fortunately acceptance and commitment therapy, as its name suggests, focuses a lot on acceptance. And as you learn to truly accept your partner's differences, you'll find your frustration, resentment, or anger starts to dissolve so you can enjoy the many pleasures that a healthy relationship can give you. (At this point, a little reminder: "acceptance" is not the only important word in acceptance and commitment therapy; there's also the word "commitment." This book is not just about acceptance—it's also about taking committed action to improve your relationship.)

myth 4: everlasting love

Does everlasting love really exist? This is a tricky question. Usually when people talk about love, they are talking about an emotional state: a wonderful mix of thoughts, feelings, and sensations. The problem with defining love this way is that feelings don't last very long. Just as the clouds above continually change—shrinking, growing, dispersing, and reappearing—so do our emotions. Thus as long as we define love as a feeling, it can never be everlasting.

Of course in the early days of a relationship, those feelings of love are more intense, last longer, and come back more quickly than they do later on. This is what we commonly call "the honeymoon phase" of a relationship, when we are totally intoxicated by those Romeo-and-Juliet, head-over-heels-in-love feelings. It doesn't last long—an average of six to eighteen months for most relationships, and rarely if ever more than three years. And when it is over, we generally experience a sense of loss. After all, it *does* feel good! So good, in fact, that when the honeymoon phase ends, many people break up with their partners, reasoning, "That's it. I don't feel in love anymore, so clearly this is not the right partner for me. I'm out of here."

This is a great pity. What few people realize is that an authentic, loving, meaningful relationship typically only develops once the honeymoon phase is over (another fact the songwriters, poets, and pop stars seem oblivious to). In the honeymoon phase, it's as if you're on a drug that intoxicates you and plays with your senses. When you're high on it, your partner seems wonderful. But you're not seeing reality; you're merely seeing a drug-induced fantasy. And only when the drug wears off do you see your partner as he really is. And you suddenly realize that the knight's shining armor is covered in rust spots, and his white horse is really a gray donkey. Or the maiden's pure silk dress is only cheap nylon, and her long golden locks are really a wig. Naturally this comes as a bit of a shock. But herein lies the opportunity to build an authentic intimate relationship between two people who see each other as they really are. And as this relationship develops, there will be new feelings of love—perhaps not as intense or intoxicating, but infinitely richer and more fulfilling.

So in view of all this, I'd like to suggest a more helpful way to think about love. Instead of a feeling, think of love as an action. The *feeling* of love comes and goes on a whim; you can't control it. But the *action* of love is something you can do, regardless of how you are feeling. For example, sometimes when my wife and I have an argument, we snap and yell at each other, get louder and louder, and eventually end the quarrel by storming off to different rooms of the house. This is not helpful or useful. It does not bring us closer together, and it does not resolve the issue; it just wastes time and drains the life from our relationship. We have learned the hard way that the sooner we can repair the damage, the better for both of us. Sometimes my wife is the first to reach out and try to resolve things—and at other times, I am. But one or the other of us will do it before long.

This is not easy. To do this, you need to open up and make room for your anger without letting yourself get consumed by it. You need to let go of all your thoughts about how you are in the right and your partner is in the wrong. You need to reconnect with your values: remember the sort of partner you want to be and the sort of relationship you want to build. And then you need to take action.

A few weeks ago my wife, Carmel, and I had a huge row, and on that occasion I was the first to reach out and attempt to make up. I was still very angry and I still believed that I was right and she was wrong, but revitalizing our relationship was more important to me than "being right." So I went into the bedroom where Carmel was reading and I apologized for yelling, and asked if she would like a cuddle. She said, "No, but if you want one we can have one." So we lay on the bed and we cuddled. But I was not feeling love for Carmel as I cuddled her. Instead I was feeling tension, frustration, anger, righteousness—and a strong urge to continue the argument and try to win it. (And Carmel was feeling pretty much the same). However, despite those strong feelings, we continued to hug each other, and eventually we both calmed down. So clearly we were both doing the *actions* of love, even though *feelings* of love were absent.

The fact that you can act with love even when you don't feel love is very empowering. Why? Because whereas the feelings of love are fleeting and largely out of your control, you can take the actions of love anytime and anyplace for the whole rest of your life. Indeed, this truth applies to all human feelings. For example, you can feel angry but act calmly. You can feel anxious but act confidently. And this ability leads us to one of the key themes in ACT: stop trying to control how you feel, and instead take control of what you do. (This emphasis on action is why ACT is pronounced as the word "act" rather than as the initials A-C-T.)

moving beyond the myths

There are plenty more love myths floating around, but these are the "big four," and you can lump them together into one massive whopper: Find the right partner, then you'll be whole and complete, and remain deeply in love for the rest of your life without any effort. For short, I refer to this story as Mission Impossible. If you believe this stuff, you are setting yourself up for a struggle with reality.

So what's the alternative? A miserable relationship where you go around acting lovingly even though you never feel it? Well, that is one alternative, but it's not one I'd recommend. My aim in this book is to help you create the best relationship you possibly can, given the limitations of reality—that is to say, a relationship in which you can act with love, appreciate what your partner has to offer, learn to accept your differences, handle your own emotions more effectively, and continue to thrive and grow until the day you die. Does that sound unbelievable? If so, good! Throughout this book, I encourage you not to believe anything just because I say so. Instead, test these ideas out and see what happens.

What I'd like you to do over the next few days is to take note of all the thoughts you have about what is wrong with your relationship or your partner. See if they are in any way connected to the "big four." Each day take a few minutes to jot some of these thoughts down in a journal, and at the end of a few days, write answers to the following questions:

- What happens to your mood when you get all caught up in thoughts of what is wrong with your relationship or your partner?

- When you buy into or dwell on these thoughts, what effect does it have on your relationship?

Note: Throughout this book, I'll be asking you to write in your journal. However, to make life easier, you might like to visit the free resources section on www.act-with-love.com. There you'll find free downloadable forms, all ready to go, for every written exercise in this book.

In the next chapter, we're going to look at what drains the love out of relationships. But before you read on, please make sure to do this exercise. Or at least think about it. That way, you'll be prepared when I ask ...

CHAPTER 2

what's your problem?

Indira: We used to have fun together—going away for weekends, having people over for dinner, partying. Now all he's interested in is watching sports on TV. I want some fun!

Greg: She seems to think I'm made out of money. Spend, spend, spend. She buys these useless bits and pieces—clothes, books, kitchen stuff. Even a new plasma screen TV. She doesn't seem to realize we have a mortgage to pay off.

Jane: He's not interested in sex anymore. He comes to bed after I'm asleep, gets up before I'm awake. I know I've put on some weight since I had the kids, but …

Demetri: She won't listen to reason. It's always got to be on her terms. She's right. She knows. My way or the highway. And if she doesn't get what she wants, believe you me—heads will roll!

Maria: He's so angry all the time. As soon as he gets in after work, he's yelling at the kids, yelling at me, complaining about everything and anything. There's no pleasing him.

Jason: She's turned into the ice maiden. She won't even let me touch her. As soon as I get near her, she's like, Get away from me!

Denise: He's never home. He's always at the office, or out with his friends, or working on his car. And when he is there, he never listens. He's always off in his own head.

Mike: Why can't she just tidy up after herself? I thought guys were supposed to be the slobs, not women! I'm always picking up after her, cleaning up. I feel like a housewife.

Do any of these complaints sound vaguely familiar? These are typical examples of the complaints I commonly hear in my counseling room. Over many years, working with people from a wide variety of backgrounds, I've heard my clients criticize their partners for just about anything you can imagine—from having bad breath to having bad taste in clothes; from having no friends to having inappropriate friends; from talking too much, to talking too little, to talking "complete nonsense." Let's face it: the number of ways in which we can find fault with our partners is almost infinite. So what's the problem in your relationship?

Are you fighting, sulking, avoiding each other? Are you having disagreements about sex, money, housework, having children, raising children, moving, changing jobs? Are you feeling lonely, unloved, rejected, put down, bullied, or henpecked? Are you bored? Are you under pressure from family, health, work, or financial issues? Are you struggling to cope with a major life challenge involving children, illness, job loss, legal action, retirement, or something else? Are you stressed out and "taking it out" on each other instead of constructively and collaboratively dealing with your challenges?

draining away life and love: five basic processes

No matter what your specific problems are, you will find there are five basic processes underlying it—five processes that are guaranteed to drain all the intimacy and vitality out of a relationship. And you can conveniently remember them with the acronym DRAIN.

D – Disconnection

R – Reactivity

A – Avoidance

I – Inside your mind

N – Neglecting values

Let's take a look at these processes, one by one.

Disconnection

Have you ever felt a special connection with someone? Presumably you did with your partner (at least in the early days, before your problems started). The word "connection" comes from the Latin terms *com*, meaning "together," and *nectere*, meaning "to bind." Thus when we connect with someone, it's as if something binds us together, unites us in some special way. When we connect with someone, we are psychologically present; in other words, we are right here with them, in this moment, fully engaged.

Obviously in order to truly connect with another human being, the first step is to pay attention to that person. But paying attention is not enough by itself. We need to pay attention with a particular attitude: one of openness, curiosity, and receptiveness. *Openness* means without defense, without hostility, without an agenda; instead of crossed arms, clenched fists, or pointed fingers, it's as if we open our arms wide to welcome the other person with a hug or embrace. *Curiosity* means a genuine interest in the other person. Letting go of our preconceived notions, we seek to learn about this person—about who they are and what they want and what they need in this moment. *Receptiveness* means a willingness to "take on board" what the other person gives us, to make room for whatever they choose to share with us.

As I mentioned earlier, paying attention with openness and curiosity is commonly known as "mindfulness." When someone connects with us mindfully, we feel important, cared for, cherished, appreciated, respected, or valued. But when someone disconnects from us; when they're withdrawn, cold, or closed off; when they're so caught up in their own thoughts and feelings that they have no interest in us; when they seem bored, resentful, or distracted in our presence; when they treat us like a nuisance, intrusion, or irritant instead of as a worthwhile human being—well, that doesn't feel very good, does it?

Unfortunately when one partner disconnects, the other often retaliates by doing the same, and soon a vicious downward spiral is established. The more you disconnect from your partner (or vice versa), the more the intimacy and warmth will drain from your relationship until eventually there is a vast, empty space between you—a dry, desolate place where life cannot thrive.

Reactivity

Bob is playing "monkeys" with his three-year-old son, Daniel. Daniel laughs with delight as Bob swings him around by an arm and a leg, making loud "Ooh, ooh, ooh" noises. It's all fun and games until that horrifying moment when Bob drops him.

Daniel hits the floor with a resounding thud. There's a brief moment of stunned silence, then he screws up his face and starts to howl like a banshee. Bob's wife, Sarah, rushes over, flustered and red-faced. "You're so irresponsible!" she snaps at Bob. She scoops up Daniel in her arms and says, "It's okay. You're okay. What did Daddy do to you?" As she pats Daniel's back, she shoots Bob an angry glare.

Bob is furious. As far as he's concerned, Sarah's reaction is totally unfair. He snaps back at her, "You are such a bitch!" and then storms out of the room.

Both Bob's and Sarah's actions are good examples of reactivity. Rather than responding to the situation with awareness, openness, and self-control, they are both running on automatic pilot. In reactive mode, we are seemingly jerked around by our thoughts and feelings like a puppet on a string; we have little or no self-awareness, and little or no conscious control over our behavior. In the grip of reactivity, we act impulsively, mindlessly, or automatically: it's as if we are driven along blindly by our emotions, blinkered by our own beliefs and judgments. The more reactive you are as a partner, the more you are likely to act in self-defeating ways that suffocate your relationship rather than breathing life into it.

Avoidance

"Hands up if you like feeling bad?" I asked. There were over six hundred people in the audience and not one single hand went up. Not surprising. Human beings do not like unpleasant feelings, and we all try hard to avoid them. This is completely natural, but it also creates problems. The more importance we place on avoiding unpleasant feelings in life, the more our life tends to go downhill. There is a wealth of scientific data to support this. Higher levels of *experiential avoidance*, the technical term for trying to avoid or get rid of unpleasant feelings, are directly linked to an increased risk of depression, anxiety, stress, addiction, and a wide variety of other health issues (Hayes et al. 1996).

Why should this be? Well, it's largely due to the strategies we commonly use for avoidance—strategies like putting stuff into our bodies, distracting ourselves, or retreating to the comfort zone. Let's take a quick look at these now.

Putting stuff into our bodies. Humans are experts at this—filling their bodies with substances to make themselves feel good: chocolate, pizza, beer, wine, cigarettes, marijuana, heroin, Valium, Ecstasy, French fries, and ice cream, to name but a few. While these substances often help us avoid unpleasant feelings in the short run, if we overrely on them, in the long run they tend to wreak havoc on our health and well-being.

Distracting ourselves. When we're feeling bad, we often try to "take our mind off it." We try to distract ourselves with anything and everything: from TV, computers, and crossword puzzles, to partying hard, burying ourselves in work, or going for a walk. While distraction helps us avoid unpleasant feelings in the short run, it is often detrimental to our quality of life. Why? First, because of wasted time. How much time have you wasted in your life watching TV, surfing the Net, or reading trashy magazines as a way to avoid boredom, anxiety, or loneliness? Imagine if you had invested that time pursuing things that were truly important and meaningful to you. Second, while we're busying our-selves in distraction, we're not taking effective action to improve our long-term quality of life. This is all too common in relationships. Rather than working on improving the way we interact with our partner, we busy ourselves in trying to feel good.

Retreating to the comfort zone. Challenging situations give rise to unpleasant feelings, such as fear, anxiety, anger, or frustration. If we want to avoid these feelings, then one way to do so is to stay well away from those situations. You may, for example, refuse to talk to your partner. Or refuse to listen to him. Or refuse to share a bed. Or you may leave the room or end the conversation as soon as you start feeling worked up. Now obviously there's a time and a place for avoiding challenging situations. For example, if a conflict starts to escalate, it may be a good idea to call "time out" and allow both of you to cool down before con-tinuing. But if you habitually run away from dealing with the challeng-ing issues in your relationship, you'll suffer in the long run.

In common parlance, we call this "staying in the comfort zone." Unfortunately the comfort zone is not that comfortable. The more you live in it, the more you feel stuck, weighed down, defeated by life. We should rename it "the stagnant zone" or the "life half-lived zone." If you want your relationship to grow and thrive, you will need to enter fully into many challenging situations and make room for the difficult feel-ings they bring. If you always avoid these situations, your relationship is doomed to stagnation.

So, all in all, avoidance is bad news for relationships. Not in mod-eration, of course. But the greater the degree to which one or both partners rely on avoidance, the more problems it's likely to create.

Inside Your Mind

Minds like to chatter. They have a lot to say that's useful and important—but a heck of a lot more that is unhelpful and unimportant. Imagine if you paid a scribe to write down every single thought that went through your mind over the next twenty-four hours: how much of it would be worth rereading? If your mind is anything like mine, very little!

When it comes to our partners, our mind is usually very quick to complain. It has an absolute ball pointing out the hundreds of different ways in which they say or do the wrong thing. And our mind loves nothing more than to take us back in time and replay all those old fights, quarrels, and grievances; to relive all those times we've been hurt or let down; to open up all those old wounds and get them bleeding again. Sometimes it takes us back to the good old days, and then it taunts us that they're all over and gone. Or it may take us into the future and show us how bad our life will be if we stay in this relationship—or how good our life will be if we leave.

Now none of this is a problem if you know how to handle your mind effectively. The problem is most of us don't know how to do this. Our default is to get trapped inside-our-mind: to give it all our attention, to take it very seriously, to believe the things it says to us, and to obey what it tells us to do. When you're inside-your-mind, you get lost in the smog of your own thought processes. And the thicker this smog becomes, the more your partner becomes a blur until you can barely see her through all your own judgments, criticisms, and grievances. And of course, when you can't see clearly, you can't act effectively.

When you're inside-your-mind, you're disconnected and reactive simultaneously. You can't truly connect with your partner because you're too entangled in your own thoughts. And you can't respond to him effectively and flexibly because you're on automatic pilot: reacting impulsively to whatever story your mind tells you. Not surprisingly, this creates all sorts of problems.

Neglecting Values

Values are your heart's deepest desires for what you want to do and what you want to stand for during your brief time upon this planet. When I ask my clients to connect with their values and tell me the sort of partner they'd ideally like to be, they often come up with words such as loving, kind, caring, generous, compassionate, supportive, fun-loving, easygoing, sensual, affectionate, and so on. In contrast, here's a list of words that *never* come up: aggressive, hostile, sulky, nagging, moody, argumentative, bitchy, untrustworthy, manipulative, lying, threatening, cold, punitive, distant.

So ask yourself this question: when things start to go "wrong" in your relationship and you start getting upset with your partner, which of these two lists has words that describe your behavior? For most people, it's the second (never come up) list. If you're not careful, as soon as you get upset, your values go out the window—and instead of being the partner you want to be, you disconnect, go into reactive mode, and get trapped inside-your-mind.

So there are five basic processes that DRAIN the life and love from our relationships: disconnection, reactivity, avoidance, staying inside-your-mind, and neglecting your values. To help clarify this, pull out your journal and jot a few notes about the DRAIN in your relationship. Look for these processes in yourself first—and only then look for them in your partner. This is important because we're very good at seeing our partner's faults but often blind to our own. (*Remember:* if you want a helping hand, you can download a worksheet from the free resources section on www.act-with-love.com.) As you continue to work through this book, keep an eye out for the DRAIN—and all the ways in which you contribute to it.

exercises to do with your partner

In most chapters from here on, you'll find a section labeled If Your Partner Is Willing. These sections contain suggestions for exercises to do with your partner. Note the word "willing" in the section name. There's no point doing these exercises grudgingly, resentfully, or half-heartedly. Unless you're both genuinely willing to do them in the interest of building a better relationship, they'll almost certainly backfire.

As you do these exercises, please don't blame or criticize or point the finger. They are an opportunity for you both to have a good honest look at what is going wrong in your relationship: how you both contribute to it and how you both can improve it. If any exercise starts turning into a fight or an argument, then stop it at once. Take a break and resume it again later, but only if you're both genuinely willing. When you discuss these exercises, it's often beneficial to go for a walk in the park or go out somewhere for a coffee or a drink. The different setting makes it easier for both partners to listen to each other without reacting negatively. Following is the first of these exercises.

---

if your partner is willing

The purpose of this exercise is to shift away from blaming, judging, and criticizing, and to look at your own role in contributing to the problems in your relationship.

exercise: *the DRAIN in your relationship*

■ Both of you make some notes on what you do to DRAIN the life from your relationship.

■ Put aside some time (ideally twenty to thirty minutes) to talk about it openly and honestly.

Soon we'll start looking at how to reverse this DRAIN through applying the principles of ACT. But first you have to answer an important question: should I stay or should I go?

PART 2

Making a Commitment

CHAPTER 3

should I stay or should I go?

I can't stand it anymore. I have to get out of this relationship.

Have you ever had a thought like that? Me too. And so has my wife. And so has almost every single one of my friends, colleagues, and family members. Is this because I hang around with a weird bunch of freakishly abnormal people? Not at all. Truth is, almost everybody has thoughts like this at times. This is the sort of stuff your mind says to you when you are going through a really tough time with your partner. And there's absolutely nothing wrong with that. In fact, it makes perfect sense when you consider how the human mind has evolved.

Think about it: how has our species—a puny naked ape—been able to take over the planet in direct competition with so many other animals that are faster and stronger and deadlier than we are? We have only managed this because of the human mind's phenomenal capacity for problem solving. The primitive mind of our distant human ancestors constantly sought ways to solve the problems of survival: how to obtain food and water, how to find shelter from the weather, and how to protect themselves from enemies and wild animals. And with each generation of humans, the mind evolved. It became more and more sophisticated until it turned into the fantastically complex problem-solving device it is today.

So now, whenever your mind encounters a problem, it immediately searches for a solution. And when a situation is painful, difficult, or threatening, then one perfectly reasonable solution is to get out of there! No wonder we think about divorcing or splitting up. But here's the thing: the solutions your mind throws up are not always wise. For example, consider all those times you've been really angry about the way someone treated you, and your mind suggested that a good solution was to yell at them or hit them or insult them. Imagine how much trouble and stress you'd have caused for yourself (and others) if you had actually followed all those suggestions. Imagine what state the world would be in if we all automatically followed every suggestion our minds ever gave us.

facing the relationship dilemma

Now obviously there are all sorts of problematic situations where getting out of there *is* the best solution—for example, when your building is on fire! But in relationships, it's rarely as clear as that, and many people struggle with the dilemma of staying or leaving. Sometimes they may even spend huge chunks of their day, trapped inside their minds, endlessly debating the issue: going over and over the pros and cons of staying or leaving. The problem is there is no vitality in this. While you are bogged down in your own thought processes, fruitlessly replaying the big debate, you are wasting huge amounts of time and missing out on large chunks of your life.

Naturally if your relationship is not good, then it's important to spend some time considering the pluses and minuses of staying or leaving. But dwelling on it day in, day out is only likely to stress you out without helping you reach a clear decision. So you may find it helpful to consider that there are basically four approaches to any problematic relationship:

Option 1: Leave

Option 2: Stay and change what can be changed

Option 3: Stay and accept what can't be changed

Option 4: Stay, give up, and do things that make it worse

Let's take a look at each in turn.

Option 1: Leave

Would your overall quality of life be better if you left than if you stayed? Based on your current life circumstances—your income, location, marital status, children (or lack of them), family and social networks, age, health, religious beliefs, and so on—is it likely that your health and vitality would be better, in the long run, if you left? Of course, you can never know this for certain, but you can make a reasonable prediction based on what has happened up to this point.

I hope you will try everything in this book—really put your heart and soul into making your relationship work—before seriously considering this option. (Obviously there may be rare exceptions to this, such as if you or your children are in physical danger from your partner, but keep in mind that this book does not deal with such serious issues.) If you do give it your best shot and you still ultimately choose to leave, then you at least have the consolation of knowing you tried your hardest to make it work. (Should this be the case, the appendix addresses how to leave your relationship in a way that minimizes damage. I hope you never have to read it.)

Option 2: Stay and Change What Can Be Changed

If you choose to stay in this relationship, the first step is to change whatever possibly can be changed to improve it. And in any situation, what you have most control over are your own actions. So focus your energy on taking action, to make things as good as they possibly can be. You cannot control your partner's actions; you can only control your own. The actions you take might involve improving your communication skills, hiring a babysitter so you can go out more, being more assertive (asking for what you want and saying no to what you don't want), or being more compassionate, affectionate, or accepting.

Keep in mind that when we talk about action, we don't mean any old action. In ACT, we encourage action guided by your values. As mentioned in the last chapter, values are your heart's deepest desires for who you want to be and what you want to stand for during your brief span on this planet. When your actions are guided by your core values, they will be very different from actions taken while you are disconnected, reactive, avoidant, or inside-your-mind.

Option 3: *Stay and Accept What Can't Be Changed*

Suppose you've taken every action possible to improve the relationship, and there's absolutely nothing more that you can do—and your relationship is still really difficult. And suppose that despite all that, you still choose to stay with your partner. If this is the choice you make, then it's time to practice acceptance. You will need to make room for those painful feelings; to let go of those judgmental, hostile, despairing or self-defeating thoughts; to catch yourself stewing and worrying. You will need to pull yourself out of that mental swampland and get back into your life. Choose to embrace your values, live in the present, and live your life to the fullest regardless of the challenges you face.

In practice, options 2 and 3 usually occur simultaneously: you take action to improve the situation, while also accepting what is out of your control.

Option 4: *Stay, Give Up, and Do Things that Make It Worse*

All too often people stay in a problematic relationship, but they don't do everything possible to improve it nor do they practice acceptance. Rather they worry, stew, ponder, analyze it to death, complain to others, obsess about it, or blame themselves or their partners. Or they become cold and withdrawn, or hostile and critical, or depressed—or even suicidal. Or they try to make themselves feel better by taking drugs, drinking alcohol, smoking cigarettes, eating junk food, zoning out in front of the TV, surfing the Internet, gambling, having affairs, shopping, and so on. Such strategies will inevitably drain your vitality in the long run. If you choose option 4, you are guaranteed to increase the suffering in your life.

sitting on the fence

You can run through these four options whenever you are stuck in a "Should I stay or should I go?" dilemma. They help you to see that you always have choices. If you typically choose option 4 as your preferred way of coping, you may find this very confronting because it forces you to take responsibility. You may even insist, "I haven't *chosen* to do this. I can't help it." If that's how you feel right now, please don't take offense or stop reading. As you work through this book and develop your psychological flexibility, you will come to see that you really *do* have a choice about how you respond to the challenges of your relationship—and you *can* choose to do so in ways that enhance your life rather than diminish it.

It's important to recognize that when you're facing the "stay or go" dilemma, there is no way *not to* choose. You can either choose to sit on the fence or you can choose to climb down from the fence—onto one side or the other. Sitting on a fence is okay for a short while, but before long, it becomes incredibly painful. And eventually, if you stay up there long enough, the fence will topple over, taking you with it! Options 1, 2, and 3 all involve getting off the fence. Option 4 is like stubbornly remaining on the fence, even though the fence posts are sticking into your flesh and you're in agony.

So given these are your only four choices, the question is—how committed are you? Let's take a look at that now.

how committed are you?

Here is a question to honestly ask yourself: on a scale of 0 to 10, where 0 means "unwilling to do any work at all" and 10 means "willing to do whatever it takes," how hard are you willing to work at improving your relationship?

If you score high, fantastic! You're off to a good start. If you score low, then take a good honest look at your situation. Do you really want to stay sitting on that fence until those posts eat through your flesh? Or can you already recognize the lifelessness in that choice?

If You Choose Option 4

At this point, you need to be painfully honest with yourself. If you're unwilling to work at this relationship, then you're effectively choosing option 4: to stay, give up, and do things that make it worse. If this is where you're at right now, then take a few days before reading on. Throughout each day, take note of the following and keep a daily record in your journal or downloaded worksheet:

- Notice the effect of "giving up" on your health and vitality.

- Notice what this choice to "give up" is costing you—in terms of emotional pain, wasted time, wasted money, wasted energy, and further damage to your relationship.

- Notice any actions you take that seem to improve your relationship or enhance your own well-being and vitality.

Now, assuming that you are committed to doing some work, the next step is to consider … does it take two to tango?

CHAPTER 4

does it take two to tango?

Chances are this is not the first material you've ever read on how to improve your relationship. And chances are some of the other stuff you've read has helped—at least in the short run. Those books and articles probably gave you some valuable insights into how your difficulties arose, and some useful tips for handling conflict, improving communication, and enhancing intimacy. And yet you probably found that in the long run, not that much really seemed to change. You soon fell back into old habits, the same old issues reared their ugly heads, and those communication skills just didn't seem to work as well in real life as they did in the transcriptions in the book—right?

I know this all too well from my own personal experience. I am an avid consumer of self-help books—I never thought I'd one day be writing my own—and I have gone through these cycles myself, over and over. Many books and articles on relationships have a strong focus on skills and techniques like these:

- Influencing your partner via effective negotiation, communication, assertiveness, and conflict-resolution skills

- Creating rituals and developing activities to cultivate affection, warmth, fun, sensuality, sexuality, intimacy, and so on

- Developing insight into the differences between you and your partner, and how they have arisen as a result of your different backgrounds

All of these are important and useful, and we will certainly touch on them within these pages. However, notice that these themes are all focused on areas of life that are out of your direct control. For example, even if you mastered all the known skills on the planet for influencing others' behavior, you still could not control them. Sorry, but there is just no guarantee that they will respond to your masterful communication, assertiveness, and negotiation skills in the way that you would like. Similarly creating rituals and developing shared activities is of vital importance for a healthy relationship, but here again it requires your partner's cooperation; therefore it is not in your direct control. So when you come to address this very important issue with your partner, here's what you will find: either he will cooperate—or he won't. There's no way you can force him to cooperate; you can only ask. Last but not least, developing insight into your differences is very useful: it enhances your own self-awareness and helps you to understand how your partner operates. But once again, it involves focusing on something outside your control; you can't alter those differences between the two of you, and you can't change the life history that has led to them. It is like understanding the weather: no matter how much insight you have into its origins and how it operates, you can't control it; you can only control the way that you respond to it.

So while we will address these important topics, they will not be the main subject matter in this book. Our aim in ACT is to help you make the most of your life—and the more you learn to focus on what is in your control, the more empowerment and fulfillment you will experience. In contrast, the more you focus on what is out of your control, the more you will feel disempowered, dissatisfied, and disappointed. This is a fact of life that we all readily forget, so I'll be reminding you of it repeatedly throughout this book.

The bulk of this book will consist of looking at these topics:

- How to stop acting in ways that make your relationship worse

■ How to clarify and act on your values and to be more like the partner you ideally want to be

■ How to accept what is out of your control

■ How to effectively handle the painful feelings and stressful thoughts that inevitably occur in every relationship

Notice that these things are all under your direct control. You can choose to stop behaving in ways that drain your relationship regardless of what your partner does. You can choose to be more like the partner you want to be regardless of what your partner does. You can choose to accept what is out of your control rather than dwelling on it or struggling with it in ways that suck the life out of you and your relationship. And once you learn how to effectively handle the stress and pain your relationship brings, you can choose how to respond when the going gets tough, which it will!

You are likely to discover a great paradox here: as you shift your focus to these areas that are within your direct control, you will often find your partner starts to make positive changes spontaneously without you even asking her. No guarantee of that, of course. But it does very often happen. And it makes perfect sense when you think about it. Imagine spending a lot of time with someone who is constantly complaining, criticizing, finding fault, pointing out the problems, and dwelling on the difficulties in your relationship. And then, all of a sudden, he changes. Suddenly she becomes a lot easier to be around. He becomes open, warm, easygoing, and willing to put all differences aside. Wouldn't you start to act differently toward a partner like this? Wouldn't your behavior change in positive ways?

Of course, this doesn't mean letting your partner walk all over you or have her way all the time. There needs to be a balance of give and take in order to keep a relationship healthy and meaningful. To make a relationship reach its highest level, both partners ideally would work on all the processes mentioned in this chapter. So yes, it does take two to tango. However, if you practice the dance steps alone, then the next time you dance with your partner, it will go more smoothly.

reality check

At this point, it's time for a reality check: no two partners will make changes to exactly the same extent. One is almost always more motivated than the other. If you cannot make room for this reality, then you will turn it into yet another problem to keep you stuck in the rut.

"That's all very well," I hear you say, "but what happens if I do all the hard work, and he makes no effort at all?" Well, if this happens, your relationship is still likely to improve, but obviously it will be a long way off reaching its full potential. So if that's what ultimately happens, then you will need to make a difficult choice: to stay or leave. But if you do choose to leave at that point, then at least you know you gave it a good try. And furthermore, you will have experienced some valuable personal growth and developed some skills that will help you in other relationships—with your friends, family, coworkers, and any future partner. On the other hand, if neither of you do any work, then your relationship is guaranteed to go from bad to worse.

so where to from here?

My assumption is that if you keep reading, then you are now committed to doing some work. Therefore the rest of this book will focus mainly on ... LOVE. Yes—you guessed it—another acronym:

L – Letting go

O – Opening up

V – Valuing

E – Engaging

Let's now explore each of these elements in more detail.

Letting Go

"Letting go" is the escape route from inside-your-mind, one of the elements that DRAIN your relationship. Your mind is like a master storyteller that never stops talking. The stories it tells you are commonly known as "thoughts." Some of these thoughts or stories are obviously true—what we call "facts." But most of the stories your mind tells you are opinions, judgments, beliefs, assumptions, attitudes, fantasies, ideas, concepts, models, interpretations, evaluations. Such stories cannot be classed as true or false; they are simply reflections of the way you see the world. Your mind will try very hard to keep you absorbed in these "stories." Your mind will dredge up painful memories from the past; conjure up scary scenarios about the future; point out all your partner's flaws and weaknesses; complain, judge, compare, and criticize; or prattle on about those love myths from chapter 1. If you hold on tightly to these stories, they will drag you down into the dark, dank depths. *Letting go* means loosening your grip on these stories. ACT will teach you how to let go of resentment, righteousness, blaming, worrying, judging, criticizing, and demanding. As you cultivate this ability, you will find you can respond far more effectively to the ongoing challenges of your relationship.

Opening Up

Intimate relationships give rise to painful feelings. And when that happens, our tendency is to do whatever we can to get rid of them or to avoid them. *Opening up* is the very opposite of avoidance. When you learn how to open up and make room for these feelings, you will find they have much less impact and influence over you, they will no longer drain or overwhelm you, and they will no longer jerk you around like a puppet on a string.

When we are in a lot of pain, we tend to shut down. We close off from our partner; we erect a thick barrier for self-protection. But this is just another form of avoidance. Sooner or later, if we want our relationship to thrive, we have to take the barrier down. And when you begin to lower that barrier, you will start to feel vulnerable. There's a good chance you will experience anxiety, worry, insecurity, or doubt: *What if I get hurt yet again?* In the past, these feelings may have held you back from making the changes necessary to rebuild your relationship. But once you can open up and accommodate these feelings, they will no longer have the power to hold you back. And there is a huge added bonus here: the more you can open up and make room for your own feelings, the more you'll be able to do the same for your partner's feelings. This is vital if you want to have a deep, intimate relationship.

Valuing

In ACT, the term *valuing* means "taking action guided by your values." Rather than neglecting values, ACT helps you to clarify them and use them to inspire and motivate your actions. Conscious values-guided action is a world apart from mindless reactivity. In this book, we will particularly focus on three core values that play a major role in healthy relationships: caring, contribution, and connection. Of course there are many others, but these three are particularly vital.

Engaging

Engaging means being psychologically present (instead of inside-your-mind) and focusing on your partner with genuine interest and openness. The more you engage with each other, the stronger and deeper your sense of connection will be—whether you're having dinner, having a chat, or having sex. Engaging means you turn toward your partner and make her the center of your attention rather than dismissing, ignoring, or turning away from her. It is the opposite of disconnection or avoidance.

could this be love?

LOVE is not just an acronym: it is a useful way of thinking about "love" itself. If you think of love as an ongoing process of letting go, opening up, valuing, and engaging, then it is always available to you—even when the feelings of love are absent. So in this sense of the word, you really can have everlasting love. But if you think of love merely as an emotion or feeling, then it can never last for long because all feelings and emotions continually change.

Practicing LOVE—letting go, opening up, valuing, engaging—will help you to drop the struggle with your partner, resolve your conflicts, settle your differences, and deepen your ability to care, connect, and bond. However, it's important to be realistic. This is not some magic wand that will miraculously fix all your issues. All couples will experience conflict and tension; that's just human nature. And when this happens, it's helpful to remember ... you're both hurting.

PART 3

Making It Work

CHAPTER 5

you're both hurting

Ever seen a movie where the hero gets punched right in the face? A gruesome slow-mo close-up, where a spray of sweat and blood flies through the air? Notice how you wince, or flinch, or turn away even though you know it's only a movie? Even though you know it's make-believe, you can't help relating to it on some level. How ironic is it that we can so easily relate to the nonexistent pain of a fictitious movie character, but we often completely forget about the very real pain of the people we love?

Humans are social animals. When it comes to affairs of the heart, most of us are pretty similar. We want to be loved, respected, and cared for. We want to get along with others and generally have a good time with them. When we fight with, reject, or distance ourselves from the people we love, we don't feel good. And when they fight with, reject, or distance themselves from us, we feel even worse. So when you fight with your partner, you both get hurt.

Your partner may not reveal his pain to you; he may just get angry, or storm out of the house, or quietly switch on the TV and start drinking, but deep inside he hurts just like you. Your partner may refuse to talk to you, she may criticize you in scathing tones, or go out on the town with her friends, but deep inside, she hurts just as you are. It is so important to recognize and remember this. We tend to get so caught up in our own suffering that we can easily forget our partner is in the same boat.

Suppose your partner has deep-seated fears of abandonment: afraid that you will leave her for someone "better." Or suppose she fears becoming trapped, controlled, or "smothered." Then when you fight, these fears will well up inside her; she may not even be aware of them because they very quickly get buried under blame or resentment. Or suppose deep inside your partner feels deeply unworthy: that he is inadequate, unlovable, not good enough. This is painful in itself, but when people feel this way inside, they often act in ways that strain the relationship. Your partner may continually seek approval, demand recognition for what he achieves or contributes, ask for reassurance that you love or admire him, or become quite jealous and possessive. If you then react with frustration, scorn, criticism, impatience, or boredom, you will reinforce his deep-seated sense of unworthiness. And this then gives rise to even more pain.

how your relationship began

Recognizing that both of you are in pain is a major step toward rebuilding your relationship. That's why, when couples come to see me, I start the first session with a little spiel. I say something like this: "Obviously you've come here to talk about the issues in your relationship and how we can resolve them, but before we do that, I'd like to know a little bit about how you met, and what your relationship was like before the problems started." I then ask them each to answer the following questions:

- How did you first meet?

- Aside from looks, what did you find most attractive about him/her?

- What personal qualities did you most admire about him/her?

- What did you enjoy doing together?

■ What did your partner do that made those times enjoyable?

■ Describe one of the most enjoyable days you've ever spent together. Where were you? What did you do? How did you interact? What sort of things did you say and do to each other? How was your body language?

■ What do you miss most about the early days of your relationship?

■ What do you see as your partner's greatest strengths?

There's a deliberate strategy here. Both partners have come to see me in a state of conflict and tension. Both are caught up in a story about what is wrong with the other. Both are hurting so much that they have likely lost touch with many of the things that drew them together in the first place. These questions momentarily connect them with some warmer, softer thoughts, feelings, and memories. As they start answering, you can visibly see them relax. Jaws unclench. Frowns disappear. They settle into their chairs. Faces soften. Instead of glaring at each other or deliberately turning away, they start to look at each other and listen. One or both may even smile, or tear up. It is heartwarming to see this happen. They have spontaneously rediscovered a sense of connection.

Alas, it doesn't always happen like that. Sometimes one partner answers in an unhelpful manner: "I can't remember," "I don't know if we ever did enjoy being together," or "We've never had an enjoyable day together. Even on our wedding day we were fighting." At other times, one partner is talking warmly and fondly, but the other is staring off into space, completely disinterested, or sneering cynically, or looking obviously bored. These simple questions, and their responses, therefore provide a wealth of information.

So take a moment now to answer those questions yourself. Turn back to the questions and ponder them quietly for a few minutes. Better still, write your responses in your journal or downloaded worksheet, and as you do so, notice what you feel:

- Can you contact any sense of warmth or appreciation for your partner? Or do you merely see him as a burden, an obstacle, a hassle?

- What happens when you take time to reflect on her strengths and positive qualities? Do you see her at all differently?

- Do you find it hard to acknowledge his positive attributes because you are so focused on his flaws and weaknesses?

Your responses will give you important information. If you can't get in touch with any sense of warmth, tenderness, or appreciation for your partner, then you're probably in a great deal of pain, with your warmth and fondness buried under layers of resentment, hurt, anger, fear, or disappointment. If so, don't give yourself a hard time. Beating yourself up will only add to the pain that's already there. Instead, take a moment to acknowledge that you are hurting. And tell yourself something kind and caring: the sort of thing you might say to your best friend if she were in as much pain as you are.

On the other hand, if this exercise does reconnect you with some warmth and tenderness for your partner, then notice how that feels. What is it like to look at your partner from a positive perspective instead of seeing him as "a problem to be fixed"?

moving on

The next thing I do in that first session is to ask each partner why they came, what they hope to achieve, and what they see as the main issue(s) with their relationship. I ask them to describe the issues as nonjudgmentally as possible—for example, instead of saying "He's a lazy slob," try saying "I have much higher standards of cleanliness than he does." This is an important first step: to start using factual descriptions instead of harsh judgments. And it doesn't come naturally for most of us. All too often, I'll have to intervene. Here's an example from my first session with Juan and Claire:

Juan: She's such a nag.

Russ: What do you mean by that?

Juan: She's always on my back. Do this. Do that. Do the other.

Russ: What's she asking you to do?

Juan: Clean up mostly. Pick up and clean up. That sort of shit.

Russ: So Claire often asks you repeatedly to pick up and clean up?

Juan: You bet she does.

Notice how I prompt Juan to move away from a harsh, negative judgment of her personality—"She's a nag"—to a nonjudgmental description of her behavior—"So Claire often asks you repeatedly to pick up and clean up?" Nonjudgmental describing is an important skill to develop. Why? Well, would you like to be described in harsh judgmental terms—such as bitch, nag, slob, lazy, dumb, selfish, mean, loser, useless—that assassinate your character? The more you see your partner through the filter of harsh negative judgments, the more you will lose touch with who he is. The person you once admired will disappear, hidden behind a wall of condemnation. So you will reap great benefits when you shift your way of describing toward being less judgmental.

On a separate but related note: while one partner speaks, I ask the other one to listen very attentively. I say, "It's hard to listen under these circumstances because no one likes to be criticized. And if you're anything like most human beings, then you will want to butt in and object or defend yourself, or put your viewpoint across or strike back with complaints or criticisms of your own. However, you're probably well aware that responding in that way is not very effective, right?" At this point, they usually answer yes. If they seem at all uncertain, I'll ask, "What normally happens when you respond in those ways?" The answer is then usually some variant of this: "We just end up fighting more, and nothing ever gets resolved."

"Uh-huh," I say. "So how about looking at this as an opportunity to learn a new way of responding to your partner: to really pay attention with an attitude of openness and curiosity instead of hostility or boredom?" In other words, I ask them to practice mindfulness. Mindful listening and nonjudgmental describing both play a role in creating a safe space, a space where both partners can start to open up and talk more freely about their difficulties. And as each partner tells their story, I will repeatedly ask them questions such as, "So when she speaks to you that way, how do you feel?" or "What is it like for you when he doesn't follow through on what he says?" or "How do you feel when she storms out of the room like that?" I do this to help them recognize how they are both hurting. To demonstrate this, here's a bit more of Juan and Claire's transcript:

Russ:　　So when Juan calls you a "nag" or a "bitch," how do you feel?

Claire:　　Furious.

Russ:　　Furious?

Claire:　　Yes! He's got no right to talk to me that way. (*Her face flushes, her arms are crossed, her voice is loud. She throws a seething glance at Juan, and he looks down at his feet.*)

Russ:　　I'm just wondering, Claire, almost always when someone is furious or angry, if we dig a bit deeper, we usually find something underneath the anger. Usually something quite painful. And I wonder if you could just check in with yourself and see if this might be the case for you. Just see if you can take a few deep breaths and kind of breathe into that anger—and see if there's another feeling, a more painful feeling, lying underneath it.

Claire:　　(*with teary eyes and wavering voice*) I feel like he hates me.

Russ:　　And what is that like? To feel like the person you love hates you?

Claire:　　It's awful.

Russ:　　(*turning to Juan*) Juan, is that what you want Claire to feel?

Juan:　　No way. (*He shakes his head vigorously.*) No way. (*He gulps heavily, his face softens, and his eyes tear up. He looks at Claire and speaks very softly, his voice cracking.*) Of course I don't hate you. I love you.

So what has happened here? Claire has dared to be open and vulnerable. She has opened up and shared some of her painful feelings with Juan. This is very different from her usual response. Normally she just shows Juan her angry exterior. In return, he becomes defensive and critical. This then makes Claire angrier and a vicious cycle results. But when Claire opens up and lets Juan see how much she is hurting, he responds very differently. He feels compassion for her: he recognizes how much she is suffering and he wants to ease it. Thus, instead of lashing out or withdrawing, he reaches out to comfort her.

Trapped inside-your-mind, you easily forget that your partner is hurting too. You get hooked by anger, resentment, and self-righteousness, and wrapped up in thoughts like these: *It's all too hard. It shouldn't be this difficult! Why won't he get off my case?* You become so focused on what is wrong with your partner, or so upset at the way he has treated you, you forget that he is a human being with feelings. You forget that he entered into this relationship for the very same reasons as you: to love and be loved, to care and be cared for, to enhance and enrich his life by sharing it with another. Neither of you entered into this relationship because you wanted to fight and quarrel and bicker and blame and judge and hurt and reject. So if you're hurting, it's guaranteed that your partner is hurting too. And as you start to recognize that you are both in the same boat, both hurting from a relationship that has turned out very differently from the way you would have liked, there comes a possibility of responding differently: with kindness and caring rather than resentment or rejection. And it doesn't take a Nobel Prize winner to know which is healthier for your relationship.

So here's what you can do now:

1. Take a few minutes to write about the major issues in your relationship. Aim to do this with nonjudgmental description rather than with harsh judgment and criticism. For example, write, "Greg does not often help out with the housework" instead of "Greg is a lazy bastard." This is difficult to do at first, so go easy on yourself. And whenever you notice a harsh judgment slipped past you, just make a mental note of it. Silently say to yourself something like, "Aha! There goes a judgment!" or "There's judging!" Then cross it out and write something nonjudgmental instead.

2. Write about the painful emotions you have experienced as a result of these issues. What painful thoughts and feelings have you struggled with? If the main feelings you notice are anger, fury, resentment, rage, or frustration, then see if you can "go deeper." These are typically surface emotions. Beneath the angry exterior, you will usually find something like hurt, sadness, guilt, shame, fear, rejection, loneliness,

inadequacy, hopelessness—or a sense of feeling unloved, unwanted, unappreciated, or neglected.

3. Acknowledge, openly and honestly, that this relationship has been painful. You have suffered. It has not been easy. You came into this relationship with all sorts of expectations, many of which have not been met. You had all sorts of dreams for the future, many of which have failed to materialize. You had all sorts of illusions about who your partner is, and many of them have been shattered. Given what you have been through, it's completely natural to feel the way you do.

4. Now this is the most challenging part: take a few minutes to reflect on how your partner has also suffered. He may never have spoken about this to you. Many men are not very good at talking about their feelings. (This is not due to a biological difference but simply because they grow up in a culture where they are not taught how to do so.) So you may have to use your imagination here. Think about what it must be like for your partner to be on the receiving end of your complaints and criticisms. If she tends to cut off, go quiet, and withdraw, then what must that be like for her—hiding away and closing down in order to cope? If she tends to brood, dwell, and rehash the past, how painful must that be for her—suffering again and again by replaying old events that can never be undone? If he gets angry and yells, then how unpleasant must that feel for him to be eaten up with anger and resentment? Surely there is no joy or pleasure involved; how much must he suffer, lost in his rage?

It is vital that you take the time to do step 4, even if it is confronting and challenging. However, your mind may try to interfere with this process; it may tell you some very unhelpful stories: *So what if he's hurting? He deserves it. He brought it on himself. Why should I care?* When your mind speaks to you this way, you have two options. One option is to get all caught up in the story and allow it to control what you do. If you choose this option, you can guarantee more conflict and tension.

The alternative option is to acknowledge the story without getting caught up in it—acknowledge it as if you've spotted an old friend on the other side of the street. Say to yourself, "Aha! I know this old story. Heard this one before." Then take a moment to reflect: "what will happen if I become deeply absorbed in this story, if I allow it to consume me?" Ask yourself, "If I give this story all my attention and allow it to dictate how I behave, will it help me to rebuild or deepen my relationship?" In doing this, you learn an important mindfulness skill: the ability to notice what your mind is saying and to choose your response—whether you clutch those thoughts tightly or loosen your grip and let go.

Acknowledging your mutual pain is a vital step in moving from conflict to resolution. When you truly recognize that you both are hurting, you will find it easier to tune into caring and compassion, both of which are essential ingredients for restoring vitality and love to your relationship.

if your partner is willing

This exercise is to help you and your partner recognize and acknowledge the ways in which you are both hurting. Hopefully it will help you develop compassion for each other.

1. Each work through all four previous steps. Once you've both done them all, read your responses to steps 1 and 2 to each other. (If you're not into writing, you can talk.)

2. As your partner speaks, practice "engaging." In other words, be mindful: pay full attention, with an attitude of curiosity and openness. Notice her tone of voice, the expressions on his face, her body language, and his choice of words. Be genuinely curious about the thoughts, ideas, or attitudes she reveals. Let go of your urges to interrupt or defend or counterattack. Listen as if you are listening to a great speech by one of your all-time heroes. Engaging fully is one of the greatest gifts you can give your partner. It is a powerful way of sending the message, "I care about you. You matter to me." But don't take my word for it: check

your own experience. How do you feel when someone pays attention to you in this manner: Special? Important? Respected?

3. Finally discuss step 4 and see how accurately you guessed your partner's feelings. You may be surprised—either by how accurate you are or by how way off the mark you are.

---

from conflict to compassion

When your best friend, a beloved relative, your child, or your dog is suffering, how do you feel? You see their pain, and you naturally want to relieve it. You want to do something kind, to help them, to support them. No one needs to teach you this; it comes instinctively. We call this "compassion." When we tune into our compassion and use it to guide our actions, we reach out and act kindly toward others.

Alas, all too often when our partner is in pain, we fail to recognize it. Or we ignore it or dismiss it. Or worse, we buy into the story that "he deserves it." Such reactions are very common, but they are also very unhelpful; they poison a relationship rather than revive it. Compassion is the antidote to this poison. Compassion doesn't alter what has happened, but it's a balm that helps the wounds to heal faster.

The first step in compassion is simply to acknowledge that your partner is in pain. She is not an emotionless shark; she is a human. And just like you, she is hurting.

The next step is to contact your natural kindness. A technique that can help you here is to picture your partner as a little boy or girl: upset, shaking, or crying. Yes, your partner has the body of an adult, but deep inside, there's a little child who's suffering. So imagine this little boy or girl in pain—and see if you can spare some kind thoughts or feelings.

You may not be able to do this just yet; you may be too hurt or too angry. If so, no problem; just acknowledge that's where you are right now, and be kind to yourself.

Over the next few weeks, whenever you are hurting as a result of some conflict, take a moment to reflect on this chapter: to acknowledge you are in pain—and so is your partner. And see if you can tune into a sense of compassion.

At the same time, find some compassion for yourself; you need it every bit as much as your partner. Over time as you do this, you'll notice a shift: a sense of your heart opening up instead of closing down. And when you notice it, enjoy it; it's one of the few pleasures in life that is free.

CHAPTER 6

everyone's a control freak!

Wouldn't it be great if your partner would do what you want? If she could only read your mind, know what you wanted, and act as you wished, life would be so much easier, wouldn't it? I like to ask my clients, "If I had a magic wand here, and I could wave it over your partner to magically transform him, what would you want to change?" Sometimes I get a flippant response like, "Well, for starters, he'd look like George Clooney!" But once they take the question seriously, there's never a shortage of answers.

How would you answer that question? Would you like your partner to be more open, loving, and affectionate? More tidy, disciplined, and responsible? More spontaneous, easygoing, and laid-back? Or would you like her to be *less* rather than more: less uptight, less serious, less needy, less of a drinker? Or would you like him to be *better* in some way: a better communicator, provider, or lover?

how we learn to control

The truth is we're all control freaks at heart; we all like to get what we want. You can see this in little children as they go through the "terrible twos." Toddlers want to get their own way, and when they don't, they may cry, yell, stamp their feet, throw themselves on the floor, sulk, hold their breath, throw their toys across the room, bite, hit, pull your hair, or shout, "I hate you, Mommy!" They'll do anything they can think of to try to control you—either to get you to back off and leave them alone, or to make you provide what they want, such as toys or ice cream.

We learn these methods of manipulation very early in life, and we never forget them. In fact, we often develop and elaborate on them as we grow older. And although we now have an adult body, that "terrible two-year-old toddler" is still inside us—and she still wants to get her own way. And even more unfortunately, when the going gets tough, we often fall back on those basic toddler tactics. We yell, snap, or criticize harshly. We swear, slam doors, thump tables, or make snide remarks and put-downs. We cry, mope, withdraw, or dole out the "silent treatment." Or, in the same way that a toddler yells, "I hate you, Mommy!" we may say all sorts of hurtful things—from nasty comparisons to ex-partners to threats of breaking up or divorce. Indeed, some adults even resort to throwing things or physical violence.

So it's time now for some honest self-examination. Put the book down and take out your journal or worksheet, and write a list of every-thing you do when you don't get your own way. List every single control tactic you have ever used—no matter how embarrassing—from fling-ing insults to flinging plates, from threatening divorce to threatening assault, from crying to spying to denying. Please don't rush through this half-heartedly. I dare you to be painfully honest with yourself.

Hopefully, when we were toddlers, the adults around us taught us an important lesson: it's a fact of life that you can't always get what you want. But knowing this doesn't stop us from trying; we are hardwired by evolution to actively strive for what we want. Without that basic drive, the human race would not have evolved to this point. Our ancient ancestors wanted more food, more water, more shelter, and more off-spring, and this drove them to invent tools and weapons, and methods for hunting, farming, and building. With each generation, our minds became more and more sophisticated, and our societies became more advanced—until we are where we are today. We now have computers, spaceships, refrigerators, cell phones, televisions, air-conditioning, cars, planes, heart transplants, and microwave popcorn.

Our incredible capacity to shape and transform our environment has created a powerful illusion of control. So much so that in this day and age, we not only have a strong drive to get what we want, we also have the expectation that we should receive it. (This expectation is further ramped up by self-help gurus who claim you *can* have anything you want if you only believe in it hard enough.) But this drive to control can be very problematic if we don't know how to handle it effectively.

do we really have control?

So let's consider: how much control do you really have in life? There are some things that you obviously have no control over: the weather, the stock market, the genes you inherited from your parents. But other things are less obvious. If you run a business, you have no control over whether your customers or clients continue to buy your products and services. Sure, you can entice them by offering great products and providing an excellent service, but it's out of your control whether they ultimately buy or not. And if you work in someone else's business, same deal: you can work hard and provide a great service, but it's out of your control whether the customers or clients are happy with it.

You can control how you drive your car, but you can't control the traffic conditions. You can control how you treat others, but you can't control how they respond to you. Builders and architects and engineers can control how they construct a skyscraper, but they can't control whether a freak earthquake topples it or an airplane crashes into it.

So what about your emotions? Can you control how you feel? Well, you've undoubtedly tried. How well did it work? Did you manage to live in a state of perpetual happiness? Did you succeed in eliminating sadness, fear, anger, guilt, embarrassment, resentment, and stress? In some situations, we do seem to have some control over our feelings—for example, if we're in a safe, nonchallenging situation like a meditation or relaxation class or listening to a motivational CD in the comfort and privacy of our car or bedroom. But the more challenging and confronting the situation, the more intense our feelings and the less we are able to control them. And let's face it—if you could control your feelings, there'd be no point reading this book: you could just make yourself feel really good about whatever happened in your relationship, so there'd be no need to work on it.

What about other people then—can you control them? Afraid not. Even if you hold a gun at another person's head, you do not control them: they can still choose to die rather than obey you. Indeed, throughout history, many courageous people have made this very choice. Think of wartime: captured soldiers or civilians who were hiding refugees chose to be shot by their captors rather than reveal information that would hurt their comrades. Of course, if a gun is placed at your head, it does have a major influence over your behavior, but it does not control you. In his amazing autobiography, *Man's Search for Meaning*, Victor Frankl, a Jewish psychiatrist who survived Auschwitz concentration camp, writes about Jews facing execution from Nazi gunmen—and he points out they could still choose to go to their death with dignity. This is an extreme example, for sure, but it's one that makes the point very powerfully.

All of these examples point to the same basic truth: the only things you can reliably control in this life are your actions. This is a very hard pill to swallow when it comes to relationships, because we so much want our partner to conform to our wishes. But this is a fact that we simply have to face if we wish to build a strong and healthy union.

---

exercise: *how I try to control my partner*

I invite you to now spend some time reflecting on everything you have ever tried doing to control your partner—and then assess how effective it was in the short run and what it cost you in the long run. The best way to do this is to draw up a table in your journal like the one shown here or download it.

What my partner says or does that I don't like	Everything I have ever said or done to get my partner to change	Did this change my partner's behavior in the long run?	Did my actions enhance and enrich our relationship in the long run? If not, what has this cost in terms of health, vitality, pain, wasted time, anger, regret, and so on?

Here's an extract from a form filled in by one of my clients:

What my partner says or does that I don't like	Everything I have ever said or done to get my partner to change	Did this change my partner's behavior in the long run?	Did my actions enhance and enrich our relationship in the long run? If not, what has this cost in terms of health, vitality, pain, wasted time, anger, regret, and so on?
He spends too much time lying on the couch, watching TV, and eating junk food	Told him he was wasting his time	No	No. My actions just created fighting, tension, and made me even more upset. Sometimes he would switch off the TV—and sometimes he'd even stop watching it for a few days—but he'd always be resentful, and the atmosphere was always very tense. It didn't bring us closer together. And sooner or later, he'd always fall back into his old ways. I've wasted a lot of time and energy getting angry about this and complaining about it.
	Called him names (couch potato, lazy slob, etc.)	No	
	Criticized him in front of friends and family	No	
	Cried	No	
	Yelled	No	
	Switched the TV off while he was watching it	No	
	Snatched the popcorn from him	No	
	Threw the remote at him	No	
	Refused to talk to him	No	
	Made him sleep on the couch	No	
	Tried to make him feel guilty by telling him he was a bad husband and father	No	
	Threatened to leave him	No	

the importance of workability

If you complete the previous form for every one of your partner's "problem behaviors," you will discover something: that what you do to try to control your partner might sometimes work in the short run to get your needs met, but often in the long run it ruins your relationship. This brings us to a very important concept in ACT: something known as "workability." The *workability* of something refers to how well it works in the long run toward creating a rich and meaningful life. Thus in ACT, we say what you are doing is workable if, in the long run, it enriches your life and enhances your vitality.

Throughout this book, I will ask you to look at what you do in your relationship not in terms of "right" and "wrong," "good" and "bad," "should" and "shouldn't," or "fair" and "unfair" but purely and simply in terms of "workability." In other words, is what you are doing working in the long run to create a rich and rewarding relationship?

Now before you angrily throw this book in the trash can, I want to clarify something. I am not suggesting for a moment that you should just suffer in silence and let your partner get away with whatever he wants. That would definitely *not* be a rich and rewarding relationship. In a meaningful, fulfilling relationship, both partners share the same attitude: we are both complete, worthy human beings, deserving of each other's respect and care and consideration, and we choose to travel down the same path in life as willing companions.

To put this more poetically, if two people want to build a fantastic relationship, each needs to be like a mountain. A mountain is whole and complete in itself—and yet when it encounters another mountain, between them they create something new: a valley. A healthy relationship is like two towering mountains with a magnificent valley between them through which the river of life flows strong and fast and free. Neither mountain needs the other—and yet their connection to one another gives rise to a lush valley teeming with the wonder of nature.

So if your idea of a partner is someone to complete you, save you, fix you, help you, solve all your problems, patch up all your wounds, meet all your needs—or alternatively someone you can fix up, save, or complete like a project—then you're going to run into problems. A mountain is strong, whole, and complete, with firm foundations and clear borders; and yet it is able to be a part of a rich and luscious landscape.

If you adopt this attitude, it does not mean you ignore or give up on your wants and desires; you, like your partner, want to be appreciated, cared for, respected, admired, and treated well. So it makes sense to acknowledge and honor those desires, wants, and needs; just don't turn them into absolute "must-haves." If you do, you'll become needy, clingy, and dependent—or critical and demanding.

There's a great paradox here. As you learn to let go of trying to control your partner, she will often start doing more of what you want. As your demands and control attempts drop off, your partner will often feel a sense of relief. This makes him more receptive to your wishes, and so more likely to spontaneously treat you well. There are no guarantees, you understand. But positive change is very common. Of course, you can and should still ask for what you want. But if you deliver a warm request, instead of a harsh or needy demand, your partner is likely to be far more responsive. (You'll discover how to do this in chapter 16).

Another bonus: when you stop wasting your energy on futile control strategies, you can invest it in becoming the partner *you* want to be. This is usually very helpful because a relationship is like a dance: as you change your footsteps, your partner will change his. Again, no guarantees here. Your partner may keep doing the same old steps, stubbornly treading on your toes. But it's far more likely that as you get in touch with your values and consciously use them to guide your actions, both you and your partner will change in positive ways. And the first step is to ...

CHAPTER 7

look inside your heart

"Can you please fix my partner?"

When couples go to counseling, this is usually their agenda. And most people read relationship self-help books with a similar intent: "This will help me work out what's wrong with my partner, and then I'll know how to fix him." This is not a helpful attitude. If you really want to make your relationship thrive, then the most effective place to start working is on yourself. So take a good look in the mirror, warts and all. Really consider these questions:

- What sort of partner are you?

- What sort of partner do you want to be?

- Is there a gap between who you want to be and the way you are acting right now?

rediscovering your values

Values are your heart's deepest desires for how you want to be and what you want to do with your time on this planet. They reflect what you want to stand for in life: how you want to behave on an ongoing basis.

Your values provide the bedrock for lasting love; neglect them and your relationship crumbles like a house with no foundation. As a general rule, the more tension and conflict we have in our relationships, the more we disconnect from our true core values. So in this chapter, we're going to rediscover them.

---

exercise: *your ten-year anniversary*

Imagine that it's ten years from now, and you have gathered together your closest friends and relatives to celebrate the last ten years of your relationship. This could be a small intimate affair in your family home or a plush affair in a fancy restaurant. It's your imagination, so make it look how you want.

Imagine that your partner stands up to make a speech about the last ten years of your life together—about what you stand for, what you mean to him, and the role that you have played in his life. Imagine him saying whatever it is, deep in your heart, you would most like to hear. (This is not about what he would realistically say—it's about what, in an ideal world, you would love to hear him say.) Imagine him describing your character, your strengths, and the ways in which you have contributed to the relationship.

Close your eyes now and take a couple of minutes to do this exercise.

What did this exercise tell you about your values? Are you truly acting like the partner you want to be? If you are sulking, withdrawing, complaining, snapping, whining, lashing out, making hurtful comments or nasty remarks, threatening, judging, criticizing, or blowing your stack—are these the behaviors you want to be remembered for?

ACT defines values as "desired qualities of ongoing action." In other words, values are about what you want to do on an ongoing basis and the manner in which you want to do it. So a value is like glue, binding together the tiniest little action to the biggest long-term goal. If you value caring for your partner, that glues together everything from holding the door open for her, to mopping her brow during childbirth, to holding her hand on her deathbed. If you value connecting with your partner, that glues together everything from paying attention to what she says, to holding hands, to having intercourse. If you value contributing to your partner, that glues together sharing the housework to paying off the mortgage to supporting a career change.

One thing to keep in mind: values are not about what you "have to do" or "should do"; they are about what is important or meaningful to you. So if words like "should," "shouldn't," "must," "have to," or "ought" start cropping up, then you are no longer in values territory: you have crossed over into ...

the land of rules

In the right context, rules are very useful. We'd be in trouble if we didn't have rules about which side of the road to drive on, or how fast we can drive, or how much we can drink before we drive. However, rules can be problematic if we hold them too tightly. We can become rigid or inflexible, and end up leading a restricted or empty life.

There are several ways you can tell when you've moved from values to rules. Values are about opening your heart and doing what is truly meaningful, so they give you a sense of lightness, openness, and expansiveness. Rules generally have a sense of heaviness about them, a sense of obligation, duty, or burden. Values tend to include words like "want," "choose," "desire," "value," "important," "meaningful," "matters." Rules tend to include words like "should," "must," "have to," "ought to," "need to," "right," "wrong," "good," or "bad."

Here are a few examples to clarify the difference:

Rule: I *have to* take my partner's needs into account.

Value: I *want to* take my partner's needs into account.

Rule: I *have to* exercise regularly, or I'll get fat.

Value: It is *important to me* to exercise regularly; I *value* maintaining my health and well-being.

Rule: I *should* spend more quality time with my partner. It's *the right thing* to do.

Value: Spending more quality time with my partner is something that *matters* to me. It's an *important* part of building the sort of relationship I *want*.

This distinction between rules and values is important for at least three reasons. First, when you live your life by rules, you will feel restricted, burdened, and stressed, whereas living by your values brings lightness, freedom, and openness. Second, there are limitless ways of acting on any value, whereas a rule massively restricts your available options. Thus values give you plenty of flexibility, whereas rules narrow your choices, and if you follow them blindly, you become rigid or inflexible. Third, it is uncommon that couples have conflicting values. Far more common, both partners have the same values, but they have different rules about how to act on them. If you hold on tightly to your rules—and insist that your rules are "right" and your partner's are "wrong"—this will readily become a source of conflict. When both of you can recognize that at a fundamental level you have very similar values, you will find this helps you to accept and respect each other.

Take the case of Janet and Mitch. Janet's elderly parents live three hundred miles away, and she would like to visit them every three or four weeks. Mitch feels this is too much; he would like to visit them no more than two or three times a year. A good starting point, in terms of resolving this issue is for Janet and Mitch to recognize that they both have similar values. They both value spending time with family, and they both think it's important to maintain healthy relationships with their relatives. The conflict arises not because of values, but because they both have different rules about how to act on them.

Knowing they share the same values provides common ground. It creates a safe space where both partners can meet, with no need to attack or defend their position. This will enable a far more fruitful discussion. From here, they can both take a look at their differing rules, consider the costs of holding them too rigidly, and discuss whether they are willing to bend them a little.

Of course, sometimes couples *do* have very different values. Let's suppose for one moment that spending time with family does not matter in the least to Mitch. Obviously this would make the situation much stickier. But if both partners tune into their values around caring, kindness, and respect while they are negotiating this issue, then the outcome will be much better.

values, valuing, and goals: giving your life direction

Values are like a compass that gives you direction: they can guide you and keep you on track during your journey. However, looking at a compass and thinking about where you want to go is not the same thing as going on a journey. In order to go on a journey, you have to get moving. So while it's important to clarify your values, it's only when you act on them that your life will improve: Taking action, guided by your values, is known in ACT as *valuing*.

Valuing is an ongoing process. It's like traveling west: no matter how far west you travel, you will never reach it. Goals are like the rivers, mountains, and valleys that you aim to cross on your journey. Thus goals can be achieved or completed, whereas valuing never ends. For example, if you want to be loving, caring, and supportive, that's a value: a desired quality of ongoing action. When you act on it, you are valuing—and when you neglect it, you are not valuing. But whether you act on it or not, that value is always there. It can't be completed or achieved; it is there, day after day, for the rest of your life. In contrast, if you want to get married, that's a goal. It can be "crossed off the list," "done," "completed," "achieved." You can achieve the goal of marriage even if you totally neglect your values around loving and caring (although your marriage probably wouldn't last too long).

Values, Wants, Needs, and Desires

Values are not the same as wants, needs, and desires. There may be all sorts of things you want or need or desire from your partner: commonly these include kindness, care, respect, tenderness, compassion, affection, intimacy, sex, and acceptance. It's important to know what you want from your partner, and in chapters 16, 17, and 18, we will look at how to increase your chance of getting it. But right now, that's not our focus. So let's be clear: your needs and desires are not the same as your values. Your values are about what you want to do, how you want to behave. They are not about what you want to get from others. To put it more simply, if you can't do it, it's not a value. So getting affection from your partner might be a want, a need, or a desire—but it's not a value. On the other hand, giving affection might be a value—or encouraging affection, or rewarding affection, or creating an atmosphere conducive to affection; these are all ongoing actions that you can *do*. There is a very good reason for focusing first on your values before addressing your wants, needs, and desires: you have total control over whether you act on your values, but you have no control over how your partner responds. So by focusing first on what is within your control, you will develop a sense of empowerment. This will stand you in good stead for negotiating with your partner.

Values: What You Want to Do

In a moment, I'm going to ask you to write about your values. But before you do so, I'd like to clarify one thing: your values are what you *want to do*. They are not about how you want to feel. If you start writing about how you want to feel—loved, cherished, supported, nurtured, respected, important, appreciated, and so on—then you're describing "emotional goals" rather than values. It's natural to want these feelings; most of us do. The problem is you have very little control over whether you get them or not. Values are far more empowering because they are always there deep inside you regardless of how you are feeling. In each and every moment, your values are accessible; they are like great friends, always on hand to help and guide you when you need them.

Also keep in mind, your values are about *you*: what you want to stand for and how you want to behave. So if you write about what you want from your partner or how you want your partner to behave differently, then those are your needs or desires but not your values.

---

exercise: *who do I want to be in relationship?*

Please pull out your journal or downloaded worksheet, and answer the following questions. And if you need some help, do Your Ten-Year Anniversary Exercise (earlier in this chapter) again.

- What sort of personal qualities do you want to bring into play in your relationship?

- What character strengths do you wish to employ or develop?

- How do you want to behave or act on an ongoing basis?

- What do you want to stand for as a partner?

- Suppose we asked your partner to describe the ten things he or she most appreciates about you. In the ideal world, what would you most love your partner to say?

What did you discover this time? Something that clarifies your values even further, I hope. Sometimes my clients get the wrong idea about this. They protest: "Are you saying I should just be all sweet and loving all the time, and let him walk all over me?"

"Absolutely not," I reply. "I don't know anyone who, deep in their heart, wants to be a doormat. I've known plenty of people who acted like doormats, but that is a surefire recipe for draining the vitality from your relationship. To make your relationship thrive, you need to look after yourself, to be true to yourself." Thus one of your main values may include being assertive: standing up for yourself, communicating your needs, asking for what you want, and saying no when appropriate. But that doesn't mean you should turn into a battering ram, yelling, insisting, demanding, criticizing, bludgeoning until you get your own way. When someone talks to you openly and honestly about your relationship with him or her—whether it's a friend, colleague, client, parent, child, or partner—how do you prefer to be spoken to? With anger, aggression, hostility, harshness, and bitterness—or with respect, compassion, care, understanding, and acceptance?

Assertiveness means standing up for yourself and taking care of your needs in a way that is respectful and caring for both yourself and others. So if assertiveness is a value of yours, write it down. Aggressiveness means standing up for yourself and taking care of your needs in a way that is disrespectful and uncaring for others: being a battering ram. Passivity means not standing up for yourself and not taking care of your needs. When you are passive, you always put others' needs before your own, no matter what the personal cost—in other words, you become a doormat. The more passive you are, the less you are being true to yourself and the more likely you are to feel tired, run-down, stressed, burned-out, anxious, or depressed, which in the long run will take its toll on both you and your partner. So both doormats and battering rams drain the vitality from a relationship. Therefore, when clarifying your values, consider self-respect and self-care as well as respect and care for your partner.

the "I'm right, you're wrong" story

Sometimes when I do these values-clarification exercises with my clients, their anger erupts: "Why are you focusing on me? *He's* the problem." Or "Hey, I'm okay with who I am. I just want her to quit bugging me."

I listen to their protests and then I ask quietly, "So you're honestly telling me that there is no way in which you can improve? Nothing you can possibly do better? That you already are the perfect partner?"

"Well, no, I'm not saying that ..." comes the embarrassed reply. And often this is enough that they start to let go of their anger. But not always. Sometimes they'll insist, "Of course I'm not perfect, but I do okay. She's the one who needs to get her act together, not me!"

In ACT, we call this the "I'm right, you're wrong" story. All of us have multiple versions of this story, and all of us get caught up in it at times. This can be very problematic. When you are convinced that you're in the right and the other person is in the wrong, what happens to your relationship with that person? Is it respectful, loving, and open? Or full of tension, conflict, and antagonism?

This is generally when I introduce the concept of workability. "How does that work for your relationship in the long run," I ask, "if you are convinced you are okay and your partner is the one who needs to change? Does it help your relationship thrive and grow?" If you are looking at your partner as a *problem* that needs to be *fixed*, you will inevitably create all sorts of tension. After all, how would you feel if someone looked at you that way?

Some of my clients still try to argue the point. "But it's true," they insist. "Just look at what he's doing!"

I reply, "In this room, I will never argue with you about what is true or false. What we are interested in is something far more important than true or false: we're interested in what *works* best for your relationship. I just invite you to notice: when you cling to the belief that your partner has to change but you don't, then—regardless of whether it's true or not—what effect does it have on your attitude and your behavior? How does it affect the way you treat your partner? In the long run, will it help your relationship?"

the foundation of loving relationships: connection, caring, and contribution

There are no such things as "right" or "wrong" values. It's like ice cream: your favorite flavor might be maple walnut, chocolate chip, or raspberry ripple. There is no right or wrong—you like what you like. If mint is your favorite flavor, there's no need to justify, explain, or defend it. Similarly your values are your values; they are what they are, and they never need to be defended or justified. (Of course, society will give you rules about how to act on your values: rules of right and wrong, or good and bad. These rules are known as "ethics," "morals," or "codes of conduct." Society will also judge some values as better than others; these are called "virtues.")

However, while there's no such thing as a right or wrong value, there are certain ones that seem essential for a rich, full, and meaningful relationship—values such as acceptance, compassion, caring, connection, contribution, fairness, kindness, respect, openness, honesty, integrity, and trust. This is by no means a fully comprehensive list; there are plenty more values you could add. However, you can also simplify this list and strip it down to three core values that form the foundation of any loving relationship: connection, caring, and contribution. If it's important to you to connect deeply, intimately, and fully with your partner; if you genuinely care about your partner's feelings, happiness, and vitality; and if you truly want to contribute to your partner's health, well-being, and quality of life, then all the other values on the list tend to follow naturally.

Caring, connection, and contribution are the building blocks of love, warmth, and intimacy, so if there's a significant lack of valuing in these areas, your relationship is likely to wither rather than flourish.

Naturally, different people use different words to express themselves; here are a few examples to get you thinking:

Connection: *I want to be intimate and close to my partner. I want to open up to him, share what I'm thinking and feeling. I want to drop the pretense, and let him know who I really am. I want to connect with him and bond with him. I want to be interested in him. I want to have fun with him. I want to see him, and allow myself to be seen by him.*

Caring: *I want to be there for my partner. I want to support her and help her. I want to show her that she matters to me. I want to act lovingly, kindly, compassionately toward her. I want to be more accepting and forgiving. I want to be friendly, warm, affectionate, understanding.*

Contribution: *I want to give my partner whatever I can to help him in life: assistance, encouragement, inspiration, or guidance. I want to offer a helping hand or a big hug whenever it is needed. I want to invest time and energy in order to aid him on his journey in life. I want to be supportive and helpful.*

Imagine what would happen if every time there was conflict or tension in your relationship, you tuned into your values around caring, connecting, and contribution. Imagine if you used caring, kindness, and respect as a foundation for discussing your issues, addressing your problems, and negotiating your needs. How might your relationship improve?

Here's one more thing to consider when reflecting on your values: what sort of character do you want to build? For example, do you want to be more open, honest, assertive, independent, communicative, cooperative, caring, loving, sensual, sexy, fun-loving, spontaneous, creative, easygoing, courageous, calm, optimistic, grateful, truthful, trustworthy, or reliable?

Now that you have a better concept of values, please go back to the last exercise, Who Do I Want to Be in Relationship? Is there anything more you can add to it?

if your partner is willing

Both complete the written exercises in this chapter. Then put aside thirty minutes to share your thoughts with each other. You may be surprised at just how similar your values are. Of course you may also discover some significant differences. If you do discover big differences, here's how to handle it.

First, don't turn this into another source of stress: "Oh no. We're so different! How are we ever going to make this work?" Recognize that these are nothing more than "differences." It's not that you have the "right" values or your partner has the "wrong" ones; you're just different. In upcoming chapters, you'll see that even if these differences are huge, you can still have a healthy relationship.

Second, recognize there are different levels of values. At a surface level, your values may seem quite different. But if you go a bit deeper, you will commonly find they are the same. For example, suppose you value playing football, whereas your partner values playing tennis. At first glance, you seem to have different values, but at a deeper level they are the same: you both value playing competitive sports. Now suppose you like playing competitive sports, but she doesn't; her favorite leisure-time activities are painting and yoga. Again, at surface level, these values seem different, but go deeper and again you'll find they are the same: you both value leisure-time activities that stimulate and challenge you.

One more example: Heath spends long hours at work and often comes home late. Shelley thinks this is not good for the kids, and she wants him to come home earlier to spend more time with them. At surface level, they seem to have different values. It seems like Heath's values are around working hard and earning money, whereas Shelley's values are around spending time together as a family. But go deeper and it turns out they both share the same values. They both want to do the best for their kids: provide for them, look after them, and help them to grow, develop, and thrive. The problem here is not different values; the problem is Heath and Shelley have different rules. Heath's rule is "work hard to buy the kids what they need." By following that rule, he can earn good money to pay for family holidays, provide clothes and toys for his children, and give them a house in a good neighborhood. Shelley's rule is "spend time together as a family." By following that rule, they can bond, have quality time, and develop richer and healthier relationships.

So if your values seem to conflict or differ greatly, then see if you can go deeper and find some common ground. This is not always possible, but it often is. Once you realize you have the same values, then you can take a look at your rules in terms of workability: if you follow these rules rigidly or insist that your rules are "right" and your partner's are "wrong," then does that attitude work to improve your relationship? Is there room for bending and modifying the rules, or holding them lightly, in order to find a better balance?

---

values: the hidden valley

Your values are like a magnificent fertile valley, stretching ahead of you, full of luscious fruit, crystal waters, and wondrous life-forms. It's pleasing to think about that valley and what you might discover there, but you'll never know what it's like unless you explore it. Valuing means you put on your boots and start walking. And as long as you're moving, every step counts, no matter how tiny.

Values-Guided Actions

Start thinking about little things you could do: simple values-guided actions to enhance your relationship. (Of course you may be feeling so hurt, angry, or resentful toward your partner that you're not willing to do these actions just yet. If that's the case, just acknowledge this is where you are right now. We'll address those issues in the next two chapters.) Following are a few ideas to get you started. Although we're focusing here on the three core values of connecting, caring, and contribution, obviously these are not the only important values in a relationship, so please add others of your own. Now please pull out your journal or worksheet and write your answers down.

Words: What can you say to your partner that promotes a deeper sense of connection or shows him that you care? How about "I love you," "I'm here for you," "Let me know how I can be of support," or "I appreciate having you in my life"? Even simple phrases such as "Thank you," "I'm sorry," or "Please forgive me" can go a long way if said genuinely. Consider text messages, cards, and e-mails as well as the spoken word.

Gestures: What actions can you take that contribute to your partner's health, well-being, and vitality? This might include anything from cooking dinner, fixing the car, or organizing a night out, to helping your partner with her chores or tasks, or giving small gifts such as flowers or CDs.

Physicality: How can you facilitate connection and caring physically? Consider hugging, kissing, holding hands, stroking hair, back rubs, sitting together on the couch, and so on.

It's Not All Sweetness and Roses

Acting on your values is satisfying in its own right. It gives you a sense of meaning, purpose, and vitality, plus the deep fulfillment that comes from being true to yourself. As a bonus, it's usually very helpful for your relationship. However, that doesn't mean that life becomes pure joy and happiness. A values-guided life also involves pain and discomfort. As you explore that valley, you will stumble at times; you'll get cut, bruised, and scraped; you'll get caught in thunder, rain, and snow; you'll get cold and wet, lost and hungry, lonely and scared. This is all part of the big adventure. There will be highs and lows, sweetness and sorrow, pleasure and pain. But you will feel fully alive. And you will know that you are challenging yourself and growing, which is surely better than wasting away in your comfort zone.

While this all sounds good in theory, there's often a problem. Frequently this magnificent valley is hidden. It is lost behind a dark, polluted cloud of anger, resentment, frustration, fear, hurt, or bitterness. This "psychological smog" is comprised of many painful stories: about what's wrong with your partner, what's missing from your relationship, and what's happened in the past that hurt or angered you. These painful thoughts and memories clump together, layer upon layer, until the smog is so thick and black that you are completely unable to see the valley beyond. In the next two chapters, you're going to study this smog—to learn how you create it and how to disperse it. In the meantime, I'd like you to try a few things and write about them in your journal or on your worksheet. Spend at least five minutes each day writing or reflecting on each of these:

- Notice those times when you are in touch with your values and acting like the partner you want to be. What does that feel like? What effect does it have on your relationship?

- Notice what happens when you get caught up in the "I'm right, you're wrong" story—or when you look at your partner as a problem to be fixed. What happens to your attitude, feelings, and behavior? What happens to your relationship? What happens to your health, well-being, and vitality?

- Start valuing. Keep it simple and easy to begin with: do tiny acts of caring, connection, and contribution. For example, you might make an unexpected phone call, or send a text message or e-mail in the middle of the day, just to say "I love you." At the end of each day, write down what you did and how it felt.

- If you don't start valuing, notice what stopped you. What thoughts or feelings got in the way?

Values-guided actions are the lifeblood of your relationship; without them, your relationship shrivels and dies. But a word of warning: if you start doing these actions primarily to get something from your partner, then you're moving away from values into needs/wants/desires/emotional goals. This is likely to create problems for you. It will set you up for frustration or disappointment. So take these actions simply because they matter to you, because they reflect what you want to stand for in life—and notice what it feels like to genuinely act as the person you want to be.

CHAPTER 8

into the smog

So you know the sort of partner you'd like to be. The question now is, what's stopping you? No doubt you would love to be more caring, considerate, kind, loving, and compassionate, but something is getting in your way, isn't it? If you want to start exploring that lush valley of your values, you need to disperse the smog that hides it from view. However, first you need to know what the smog is composed of. The following questions have been designed to help you do that. So take out your journal or worksheet, and as we come to each question, please write down as detailed an answer as possible.

Suppose a miracle happened and your partner suddenly turned into your perfect "soul mate": no faults at all, no annoying habits, always there for you, able to meet your every need, want, and desire.

- If that happened, then how would *you* change?

- What would you stop, start, do more of and less of?

- What sort of partner would you try to become?

- What sort of personal qualities would you develop?

- What attitude would you cultivate toward your partner?

■ How would you respond to him when he's in pain? How would you treat her when she made a mistake or screwed up?

So what did you learn about yourself? Did you discover a gap? A gap between the way you'd ideally behave and the way that you actually do behave? If you did notice a gap, that's a good sign. It means you are a normal human being. And the more stressful and challenging your relationship is, the larger this gap will tend to be. Hopefully over time you'll be able to bridge that gap, but the first step is simply to notice it's there.

At this point, notice what your mind is telling you. Most people find that as soon as they become aware of the gap, their mind starts trying hard to justify it. Common justifications include, "I wouldn't be acting this way if he would just do X, Y, and Z" or "If she would just stop doing *that*, then I wouldn't have to do *this*." While such thoughts are normal, they are not particularly helpful. Justifications are just one of the many layers in your psychological smog that hold you back from the great adventure of valued living. The next four questions will help you uncover some other layers (write your answers now):

■ What is stopping you from living by your values right now?

■ What do you fear might happen if you did start to live more by your values?

■ What do you think needs to happen first before you can start living more by your values?

■ Do you believe your partner should change before you do? If so, what do you expect your partner to do?

layer upon layer of psychological smog

Your psychological smog is a potent, toxic blend of unhelpful thoughts, scary predictions, rigid attitudes, harsh judgments, and painful memories. Over the years, they have built up, layer upon layer, into a thick black cloud that suffocates and smothers you, and prevents you from living the life that you truly want. If you answered the previous questions, in all likelihood you discovered some or all of the following smoggy layers:

The Should Layer

This layer is made up of thoughts such as these:

■ Why *should* I bother?

■ It's not my problem; I *shouldn't* have to change.

■ Why *should* I make it easy for him?

■ She *shouldn't* have treated me that way.

■ He *should* apologize and admit he's wrong.

■ It *shouldn't* be this hard.

When we get caught up in these thoughts, we become righteous, indignant, angry, or resentful. The word "should" implies there is a rule that must be followed. If our partner does not follow the rule that we have proclaimed, inevitably we get upset. Take a moment to reflect on this question: What does your mind say your partner should do? He should know what you want? She should respect your wishes? He should put his clothes away? She should approve of your friends? He should spend more time on foreplay? She should have more interest in sex?

It's perfectly natural to think this way. Your mind is like a "should factory": it churns out those "shoulds" in a never-ending stream, in all sorts of shapes and sizes. You may insist, "But it's true; he should put his clothes away." But true or false is not the issue here; it's all about workability. How does it work for your relationship when you get all caught up in these "shoulds"? Doesn't it just ramp up your resentment? Doesn't it just increase the tension and conflict?

The No Point Trying Layer

This layer is made up of beliefs that the future is all doom and gloom, so there's no point trying. Here are two examples:

- It's too late. There's too much damage. We can never repair it, so why waste my time?

- She'll never change, so why should I make the effort?

Do you ever have thoughts along these lines? Most people do, especially when the going gets tough. But what happens if you let these thoughts push you around? What happens to your relationship if you give up?

The If Only Layer

This layer is composed of wishful thinking:

- If only he would get his act together ...

- If only she would get off my back ...

- If only he would share his feelings more openly ...

- If only she could get on better with my parents ...

We all get caught up in wishful thinking at times. It's a temporary escape into fantasyland. Alas, the more time you spend in the land of "if only," the more discontented you become with the land of "reality." If you're not careful, you can spend hours lost in this sort of smoggy thinking. And does it help you, in any long-lasting way? Does it improve your relationship in any way, shape, or form?

The Painful Past Layer

Here you've got all those painful memories of everything that has ever gone wrong in your relationship: the million and one ways in which your partner has screwed up, hurt you, or let you down. Most of us don't have to try too hard to recall them; as soon as things get tense, our mind conveniently turns on its own DVD player, and cranks up the sound to full volume. And all too readily we sit down to watch those old movies, even though nothing useful ever comes of it. Don't take my word for this: check your experience. Has dwelling on painful memories ever been useful for your relationship? Or does it just feed into resentment and righteousness? Doesn't it just increase your discontentment?

The Scary Future Layer

This layer is made up of all the scary thoughts we have about what might go wrong if we *do* change:

- She'll take advantage of me.

- I'll get hurt.

- He won't take responsibility.

- She'll never change.

- He'll just do it again.

- She'll take me for granted.

- I'll be stuck in this relationship, and it'll just get worse.

- I'm making the wrong choice; I'd be happier with someone else.

- If I don't leave now, I'll be too old to find someone more suitable.

Most of us have a tendency to imagine scary scenarios about the future. There's nothing unusual about that; it's a result of evolution. Our primitive ancestors needed to anticipate danger. If they didn't do this well enough, they got eaten. The better they could predict and prepare for danger, the longer they lived and the more offspring they had. Therefore, with each generation, the human mind became better at anticipating threats. And as a result, our modern-day mind now does this all the time: it constantly looks out for anything that might harm us or hurt us. Unfortunately this tends to manifest as "worrying," "stressing out," or "imagining the worst."

Here's one of the most compelling of these scary stories: "If I change, my partner will take advantage of me. I'll be doing all the hard work; I'll be giving, giving, giving, and he'll just be taking." This is a very common and completely normal fear—all the more so if your partner already has a record for this sort of thing. The problem is, if you buy into this story, it keeps you stuck. You've probably tried the waiting game already: refusing to change unless he changes first. So how did that work for you? The only surefire way to get unstuck is for you to be the one who makes the first move. So why not try it? If you do make the first move and your predictions turn out to be accurate—well, it's very disappointing, but at least you know you tried. If you don't even try, then you know exactly where your relationship is headed. (And don't expect your mind to play ball. Expect your mind to keep on telling you this story; it knows it's an easy way to grab your attention.) So now take a moment to reflect on the following questions:

- What are the scariest stories your mind likes to tell you?

- When you get caught up in these stories, does it help you take action to improve your relationship? Does it help you grow closer to your partner?

- Does getting caught up in these stories hold you back from making important changes? Does it feed your desire to give up or run away?

The Reason-Giving Layer

This layer is made up of all the reasons we come up with for why we can't or won't change:

- I'm too depressed/stressed/tired/run-down.

- I've had enough. I've got no energy left to try anymore.

- I'm happy with who I am. She needs to change, not me.

- I'm too old to change.

- I've always been this way. This is the way I am. Take it or leave it.

- I just don't care anymore.

- If he changes first, then I'll change!

Our minds are brilliant at reason giving. But reasons are almost always just "excuses." And in the short run, they're convenient: they help us avoid the discomfort of hard work. But do they help you in the long run? If you get all caught up in these excuses—if you latch on to them tightly and allow them to dictate your actions—then what is the long-term effect upon your relationship?

The Judgment Layer

This one comprises all the negative judgments we make about our partner:

- He doesn't deserve to be treated well.

- She's a bitch. Why should I be nice to her?

- He's a loser. He doesn't deserve my respect.

- She's too aggressive; that's her problem.

- He's the one with all the issues, not me.

Take a moment here to reflect: what sort of judgments does your mind make about your partner?

- When your mind really wants to do a "hatchet job"—to cut your partner into tiny little pieces—what are some of the nastiest judgments it makes? What are some of the nastiest names it uses? Selfish? Slob? Bitch? Bastard? Psycho? Asshole? Depressing? Weak? Arrogant? Egotistical? Spiteful? Jealous? Manipulative? Self-indulgent? Disgusting? Control freak?

- What happens to your relationship when you get absorbed in thoughts like these? Are these the sort of thoughts you want to hold on to? How do you feel when you get entangled in them?

- If you allow these thoughts to dictate your actions, does that help you to repair or strengthen your relationship?

The I Know Why Layer

This layer is made up of assumptions. You analyze your partner and try to figure out why she keeps doing these things: why can't she just stop? Your mind comes up with all sorts of plausible ideas: her unconscious motivations, her hidden desires, her secret agendas. Minds can be endlessly inventive with this stuff. Take a few moments to reflect: what stories has your mind invented to explain your partner's behavior? Do any of these ring a bell?

- She's doing it on purpose, to prove a point.

- He's doing it to hurt me.

- She could change if she really wanted to. She just can't be bothered.

- He's got an unconscious hostility toward women.

- It's because deep down inside she wants to leave me.

It's certainly a fascinating game, analyzing your partner. And the results can seem very convincing. But what happens when you treat those assumptions as facts? If you hold on to these explanations and treat them as the literal truth, does this help you build a better relationship?

Deep-Seated Fears

Deep-seated fears can often get in the way of our values. Three of the most common are fear of abandonment (that your partner will leave you), fear of control (that your partner will smother you, control you, intrude on you, or even overwhelm you with demands for love and affection), and fear of unworthiness (that you are inadequate, unworthy, unlovable). These deep-seated fears may surface as utterly compelling stories such as these:

■ He's going to leave me. I couldn't bear to be without him.

■ I'm not good enough for her. I know she'll find someone better.

■ He's trying to control me. He won't let me be who I am.

■ If I give her what she wants, there'll be nothing left of me.

■ When he finds out what I'm really like, he'll leave.

When you hold on tightly to thoughts of abandonment, what happens? Do you become clingy, needy, jealous, possessive? Or do you start to act like a "doormat" and lose touch with your values around self-respect and self-care, too afraid to ask for what you want in case your partner disapproves? And if you get caught up in stories about control, what happens then? Does it help you to bond with your partner, or does it increase the distance between you?

see anything you recognize?

Do you recognize any of the thoughts just listed? Most of us have at least some elements of this smog swirling around inside our heads. And some of those smoggy thoughts may be absolutely true. But remember in ACT, we are not so much concerned with what is true as what is helpful. In other words, if you get caught up in these thoughts and allow them to control what you do, will that help you to create a rich, full, and meaningful relationship?

Now you can't stop these thoughts from showing up. I'm assuming you've already discovered that for yourself. If not, then don't take my word for it: check it out for yourself. Try to stop your mind from having these thoughts. Try to think nothing but positive thoughts—and see how long you last before a negative one appears. Or try to push those thoughts out of your head—and notice just how quickly they come bouncing back. Or try to challenge them—and notice how much time you waste, embroiled in a debate with your own mind. (And if you should actually win that debate temporarily, just notice how quickly those very same thoughts reappear; they won't remain defeated for very long.)

Of course you may find that these thoughts give you a break at times—when you're in a great mood, or you're on vacation, or your partner is on her best behavior—but you've undoubtedly discovered that as soon as your mood takes a downturn, or your stress levels increase, or your partner's behavior lapses, those thoughts immediately spring back into action. And some of those thoughts are very old, aren't they? Some of them have been around since the early days of your relationship. Some of them have even been present in other relationships. (I'm not a mind reader, by the way; this is how it is for almost every human being on the planet, so I'm assuming you're "one of us.") So given you cannot stop these thoughts from reappearing, how will you respond the next time they show up?

One response is to let yourself get caught up in them: give them all your attention and treat them as if they're the absolute gospel truth. If this is how you respond to your thoughts, does it help you to be the partner you want to be or to build the relationship you want to build? If you dwell on them, stew over them, replay them silently inside your head, or replay them aloud to other people; if you give them all your attention, latch on to them, get completely immersed in them, then what happens to your behavior? What happens to your values? What happens to your relationship?

Remember the DRAIN? When you get sucked inside-your-mind, you will disconnect from your partner, become reactive, and neglect your values. In itself, that's not hard to understand; here's the really tricky part:

> It is *not* your thoughts themselves that create the smog.
> They only turn into smog if you *hold on to them!*

It is important to recognize this. If your thoughts were creating the smog, then the only way to disperse it would be to get rid of them. But as we have already discussed, there is no way to permanently get rid of these thoughts. You may be able to push them away for a while, but sooner or later they will return. So how then are you supposed to disperse the smog? By learning how to let these thoughts come and go instead of getting all caught up in them. By holding them gently like a butterfly in the hand instead of clutching them tightly like a ten-dollar bill. By learning to see them for what they are—nothing more or less than words popping up inside your head. By allowing them to come and go freely as if they were merely cars driving past your house. When you hold on to these thoughts, they build up, and when you loosen your grip, they disperse. This is what we mean by "letting go," and in the next chapter, you'll learn about how to do that. But first, experience for yourself how to create smog.

---

exercise: *how to create smog*

This exercise shows you what happens when you hold on tightly to your thoughts. Pull your journal or worksheet out once again, and write down as many "smoggy" thoughts as you can identify. Using the previous examples as a guide, write your thoughts under the following headings:

Shoulds

No Point Trying

If Only

Painful Past

Scary Future

Reason Giving

Judgments

I Know Why

Deep-Seated Fears

Okay, so now you've got a long list of "smoggy thoughts." The next step is to read them through and buy into them as much as you can. Give them all your attention, dwell on them, believe them, get totally absorbed in them. The aim is to make the smog as thick as it can possibly be, to get so absorbed in these thoughts that you basically lose touch with everything else. Do this for at least a minute.

Now check in and see how you are feeling. When we get lost in the smog, we soon stumble into the quicksand of painful emotions. Are you feeling hurt? Angry? Resentful? Lonely? Sad? Righteous? Anxious? Depressed? Contemptuous? Disgusted? Hateful? Frustrated? Annoyed? Tearful? Furious? How do you feel toward your partner right now? Do you feel close and connected to him—or distant and disconnected? Does dwelling on these thoughts help to remove the wall that has grown between you? Or does it make that wall even thicker? Right now, do you feel like you want to act on your values—to care for and connect with your partner? Or do you feel more like giving up, running away, or lashing out?

if your partner is willing

Both do this exercise, then make time to talk about it openly. You may be surprised to find that many of your smoggy thoughts are similar. Discuss whether they are brand-new thoughts or old ones. Are they just variants of old stories that have been showing up for years? Have they ever shown up in other relationships, not just with partners but also with friends and family?

---

losing touch

Hopefully you can see that the more you get entangled in these thoughts, the thicker the smog gets. To really get this concept, hold your journal or worksheet up in front of your face so that it's touching the tip of your nose. Now what happens to your view of the room? You can't see anything, right? If your partner were standing directly in front of you, you wouldn't be able to see her. All you can see are your own smoggy thoughts. When we get caught up in this psychological smog, we lose touch with two very important people:

Our partners: Our vision obscured by smog, we can no longer see them as they really are.

Ourselves: Smothered by the smog, we are lost—wandering blindly, our values all but forgotten. The thicker the smog, the more out of touch we are with who we really want to be.

Psychological smog is a major DRAIN on our relationships; caught up in it, we disconnect, become reactive, avoid our partner, get lost inside-our-mind, and neglect our values. If we want to disperse this smog, we must first learn how to handle ...

CHAPTER 9

the judgment machine

Incompetent! Idiot! Fat! Ugly! Boring! Fake! Selfish! Greedy! Manipulative! Arrogant! Judgmental! Nobody likes you! You're a lousy father! You're getting old!

Q: What do all these words have in common?

A: They are all things my mind says to me when it wants to beat me up and bring me down.

Now some readers may be gasping at this point: "What is this? This guy's writing a self-help book and he thinks like that about himself?" Well ... it's not quite as simple as that. Yes, at times those thoughts do pop up inside my head—usually when I've screwed up or acted out in some way that is totally out of keeping with my values. But the point is, when those thoughts do pop up, I don't usually buy into them. I rarely get caught up in them or take them seriously. Most of the time when those thoughts show up, they don't bother me; they're like water off a duck's back. My mind can scream abuse at me, and it has no more impact than a radio playing softly in the background. How is this possible? Thanks to a key ACT process called "defusion."

Before we take a look at defusion, let me ask you this: does your mind ever say things like this to you? I'm willing to bet it does. I give workshops to literally thousands of people every year, and I always ask the audience, "Is there anyone in the room today whose mind does not have some version of the 'I'm not good enough story'? Anyone here whose mind does not, at times, tell them a story about what is wrong with them, what they are lacking, what their faults are? If so, please raise your hand." To this day, no one has ever raised a hand!

---

exercise: *the judgmental mind—part 1*

So what does your mind say to you when it really wants to beat you up? When your mind turns into judge, jury, and executioner—when it lays out all the evidence about what's wrong with you, judges you as not good enough, and sentences you to suffer—what does that sound like? If I could listen in to your thoughts, what would I hear your mind saying?

Take a moment to jot down some of the things your mind says. You can write in this book, download a worksheet, or record your responses in your journal. Complete each sentence with as many words or phrases as you can think of.

When my mind wants to judge me as "not good enough," this is what it says:

- My mind tells me that I am a …

- My mind tells me that I am too …

- My mind tells me that I am not enough of a …

- My mind tells me that I do too much of the following:

- My mind tells me that I don't do enough of the following:

- My mind tells me that I lack the following:

Once you've done that, read through the list, pick the self-judgment that bothers you the most, and shorten it to a simple phrase of no more than five or six words—for example, I'm a loser, I'm too selfish, or I'm not witty enough.

Done that? Okay, now I'm going to ask you to do a few things with that judgment. First, I'm going to ask you to buy into it, give it all your attention, believe it as much as possible. "What? Are you crazy?" I hear you ask. "I don't like these thoughts. Why are you telling me to believe them?" Let me reassure you, there is an important point to this. Obviously buying into these thoughts is likely to make you feel a bit yucky, but I'm hoping you'll be willing to do it for a few seconds in order to learn something really useful: how to practice "defusion," the important ACT process I mentioned earlier. So here goes …

Bring to mind your negative self-judgment—in the form of "I am X"—and buy into it as much as you possibly can for twenty seconds. Notice what happens.

Now silently replay that judgment in your head, word for word the same, but this time put a little phrase in front of it: "I'm having the thought that …" Notice what happens.

Now do that again, but the added phrase is now slightly different: "I notice I'm having the thought that …" Notice what happens.

So what happened? When they add the phrase "I'm having the thought that …" or "I notice I'm having the thought that …," most people get a sense of separation or distance from their self-judgment. The thought doesn't go away, but it loses some of its impact. This process is called "defusion." Why? Well, think of two metal sheets fused together. If you couldn't use the word "fused" to describe them, what word would you use? Joined? Stuck? Bound? Melted? Welded? All of these words imply the same thing: that there is no separation; those sheets of metal are completely stuck together. In ACT, we talk about "fusion" with your thoughts: a technical term that means you get caught up or entangled in your thoughts. *Defusion* means separating from your thoughts, getting some distance from them, stepping back and watching your thoughts instead of getting lost in them.

defusion: getting unstuck from your thoughts

If we go back to DRAIN (disconnection, reactivity, avoidance, inside-your-mind, neglecting values), then fusion means getting trapped inside-your-mind. And *defusion* is the way we escape from that trap. Defusion involves "taking a step back" from your mind: noticing the story your mind is telling you rather than getting absorbed in it. In a state of *fusion*, you are lost in your thoughts; in a state of *defusion*, you can step back and watch your own thinking, and choose how to respond to it.

---

exercise: *learning how to get unstuck*

This exercise will help you step back and watch your own thinking. Stop reading for twenty seconds, close your eyes, and just notice what your mind is telling you.

Now do that again, and this time see if you can notice the *form* that your thoughts take: are they pictures, words, or sounds?

Now do that one more time, and this time see if you can notice where your thoughts seem to be located. Do they seem to be in front of you, behind you, above you, to one side of you, inside your head, or inside your body? And are they moving or still?

Doing those little exercises helps us to defuse from our thoughts: to separate from them a bit, get some distance from them, have a look at them. If we want to build meaningful relationships and improve our life in general, it is essential that we learn how to do this. Why? Well, here's an exercise that will make the point more effectively than just describing it.

---

exercise: *if your hands were your thoughts*

Imagine for a moment that your hands are your thoughts. Rest this book on your lap or on a table so you can free up both your hands to do this exercise. Place your hands side by side, palms upward, as if they are the pages of an open book. Hold them out in front of you. Notice that you can see your hands clearly, and you can also clearly see the room around you.

Now, once you have finished reading this sentence, I'd like you ever so slowly to raise your hands up toward your face until they are both touching your face and completely covering your eyes—and then notice what has happened to your view of the room around you.

What did you notice? You could probably see bits and pieces of the room through the gaps in your fingers, but most of the room disappeared from view. This is what happens when we fuse with our thoughts: we get so caught up in them, we lose touch with the big picture. Now suppose your hands represent all the negative judgments you make about your partner. And suppose your partner is standing right in front of you. What happens to your view of your partner as you bring your hands up right in front of your face? That's right: the closer your hands get to your face, the less clearly you can see your partner until at last you can only see a few tiny bits of him through the gaps in your fingers.

This is exactly what happens when we fuse with negative judgments. We get so caught up in our stories about what's wrong with our partners, we no longer see them as they are. All we see are the labels our mind has slapped on them: loser, selfish, lazy, uncaring, slob, bitch, incompetent, untrustworthy, liar, overemotional, difficult, and so on. We lose touch with the fact that there is a whole person in front of us—a person with many different facets of personality and a wide range of strengths and weaknesses. Instead we see our partner through a filter of criticism and condemnation, and then—surprise, surprise—we end up dissatisfied and discontented.

"Yes, that's all very well," I hear you say, "but what if those judgments are true?" Good point. Remember, in ACT, everything boils down to workability. It's not a question of whether your judgments are true or false—it's a question of how it works *in the long run* if you fuse with them. What impact does it have on your relationship? If you choose to stay in this relationship and make the most of it, then will fusing with those judgments increase or decrease your satisfaction?

Quickly do this little exercise again—and this time, notice that while your hands are covering your face, it is difficult to act effectively. Imagine trying to drive a car or chop vegetables or type on a computer with both your hands in front of your face! Similarly it is difficult for you to act effectively, according to your values, when you are blinded by all your judgments about your partner. But if you can defuse from all those judgments and tune into your values, you will notice a big difference.

For example, suppose you want your partner to help out with the housework. Your mind instantly starts telling you the "bad partner" story. It says something like, *He's so lazy and selfish. Why doesn't he ever do any housework? I shouldn't have to ask him. What am I, his slave?* Now what happens if you fuse with that story? Right, you snap at him or you say something nasty. Or you try asking him nicely, but it comes out laden with scorn, contempt, anger, or bitterness. Or you say nothing; you just do it yourself—but you do so full of resentment.

Now just suppose you could defuse from that story. Suppose that, instead of getting caught up in it, you could put it to one side and connect with your values around assertiveness, acceptance, and friendliness. The smog lifts, and there is the lush valley stretching in front of you. You could then accept that your partner is different from you, and therefore has different attitudes and habits than you. And you could remember that he is your friend instead of your foe. And you could remember how you like to treat your friends. You could also practice being assertive, which in this instance means asking for what you want while respecting your partner's right to be spoken to politely. So you could then say, without anger or bitterness, "I'd really appreciate it if you could help me with tidying up a little." Of course there is no guarantee your partner will help out, but he is far more likely to do so when asked in this way—and to do so willingly rather than resentfully. For sure, snapping and criticizing might also prompt him to help out, but in those instances he would probably be doing so with bitterness or resentment, which is not good for your relationship in the long run.

Can You Stop Your Mind from Judging?

The only way I know of to stop your mind from judging is to do some major brain surgery and chop out all the bits responsible for thinking. But don't take my word for it: try it yourself. Set the timer on your watch, go for a quick walk, and see how long you last before your mind starts making a negative judgment about someone or something. I'm willing to bet it won't take too long. And there's no need to feel guilty about this. It's completely normal and natural. Thanks to evolution, the modern human mind is a precision-engineered judgment machine that never rests.

You see, the mind of our primitive ancestors needed to make important judgments continually in order to survive in a dangerous, hostile world. A figure in the distance: friend or foe? An animal in the bushes:

dangerous or harmless? A steep rocky path up the mountain: safe or unstable? So if the primitive mind of our ancestors had not been good at making these judgment calls, they would not have survived long enough to reproduce and pass on their genes. Thus now, as a result of countless eons of evolution, we have minds that never stop judging. And what this means is that along with all the useful words the judgment machine churns out, there are also a lot that are useless or downright unhelpful. So what do we do with all this stuff?

Calling a Spade "a Spade"

There are many different ways of defusing from unhelpful judgments and stories about your partner. One way is simply to name them whenever they show up. As soon as you notice the judgment machine is spewing out its stuff, you can silently say to yourself, *Aha! Judgment time again*. Or, *Ha! Here's the "bad partner" story. I know this one*. The moment you do this, you are starting to defuse from the story instead of getting trapped in it. Defusing from the "bad partner" story does not come naturally, but with practice it gets easier. You might also like to give your "bad partner" story a specific name—for example, The Lazy Slob Story or The Workaholic Story. Then each time you notice yourself getting hooked in by a thought or feeling that is connected to that story, you can name what is happening: *Aha! The Workaholic Story. There it is again*.

Here are some light-hearted phrases you might play with: "Judgment Day—again!" "Aha! The judgment machine's on red alert." Or more simply, "Here's judging." I invite you to play around with this over the next few weeks. See if you can catch the judgment machine in action, label what it is doing, and notice what happens. *Remember*: The aim is not to stop the judgments; there's really no way to do that. The aim is to see them for what they are: just a bunch of words that are automatically churned out by your mind.

I'd like you now to do part 2 of the Judgmental Mind Exercise. This time you're looking at judgments about your partner rather than judgments about yourself. Complete each sentence with as many words or phrases as you can think of.

exercise: *the judgmental mind—part 2*

When my mind wants to hook me into the "bad partner" story, this is what it says:

- It tells me that my partner is a ...

- It tells me that my partner is too ...

- It tells me that my partner is not enough of a ...

- It tells me that my partner does too much of the following:

- It tells me that my partner doesn't do enough of the following:

- It tells me that my partner lacks the following:

Now read through the list and pick the judgment that bothers you the most and simplify it into this format: "My partner is X" or "My partner is not Y."

Now hold that thought in your mind and buy into it as much as you possibly can for twenty seconds. Notice what happens.

Now silently replay it in your head, word for word the same, but this time put a little phrase in front of it: "I'm having the thought that ..." Notice what happens.

Now do that again, but the added phrase is now slightly different: "I notice I'm having the thought that ..." Notice what happens.

How did you do? I hope you defused from it a bit. If not, try it again with a different judgment from the list.

exercise: *carrying your judgments*

Here's a different defusion exercise. First find a blank sheet of paper. It needs to be a loose sheet, so if you're using a journal or notepad, tear a page out of it. On one side of the sheet, write down four or five of the harshest judgments or stories that your mind tells you about your partner. (To make this easy, you could just copy your answers from the Judgmental Mind—Part 2 Exercise but leave out the phrase "It tells me that ...")

Once you've done that, turn the sheet over and write in large bold capitals: AHA! THE BAD PARTNER STORY. THERE IT IS AGAIN! (Obviously, change the name of the story if you can think of a better one.)

Now turn the sheet back over again and read through the list of all your judgments and stories. Once you've done that, flip the sheet over and read the bold capitals on the back. Notice what happens.

Did you do it? If not, please give it a try. Most people find it instantly helps them to defuse. Once I've taken my clients through that exercise, I ask them, "Would you be willing to fold that piece of paper up for the next week, carry it around with you in your purse or wallet, and pull it out four or five times a day, and repeat the exercise: first read through all the judgments, then flip it over and read what you've written on the back?" I encourage you to try this yourself. While there are no guarantees with any of the techniques in this book, most clients report a week later that they are defusing from the "bad partner" story much more easily and not getting caught up in it as often.

---

if your partner is willing

I'll finish this chapter with a variant of the previous exercises, especially designed for couples. If your partner is willing, you can do this together. If not, then just imagine it as vividly as you can. Here's how I run it during a counseling session:

Each partner fills in a sheet of paper on both sides, exactly as in the last exercise. Then I ask them to stand opposite each other and hold the sheets of paper right in front of their faces so all they can see is a list of their negative judgments. I then ask them to talk to each other for a few seconds. Next I ask, "What is it like to do this? Do you feel connected with each other? Can you read each other's expressions? Do you feel engaged, close, intimate?"

Next I ask them to tuck their sheets of paper under their arms and again talk to each other for a few seconds. "Now what is that like?" I ask. "Do you feel more connected?" The answer is always yes.

Finally I point out, "You haven't gotten rid of those judgments—they are still with you—but you have changed the way you are interacting with them." This is a key aspect of defusion: it's not a way to get rid of unwanted thoughts—it's just a different way of interacting with them.

---

practice, practice, practice

You can't learn to drive by reading a book about it; you actually have to get in a car and practice. The same goes for all the psychological skills in this book. So, if your relationship matters to you, are you willing to practice the following?

- Do the Carrying Your Judgments Exercise as described previously. Carry the folded paper around in your purse or wallet, and pull it out at least four times a day. Read the list of judgments, then flip it over and read the bold capitals on the back.

- Throughout the day whenever you catch your mind judging, silently label it with a phrase like, *Here's judging,* or *Aha! The "bad partner" story,* or, simpler still, *Judging.*

- The moment you realize you've been hooked by an unhelpful story or judgment, try defusing from it with a phrase like, "I notice my mind is judging that …" or "My mind's telling me the story that …" or, simpler still, "I'm having the thought that …"

Play around with the phrases I've suggested. Change them into your own words, and notice what happens. See if that psychological smog starts to disperse. And if it doesn't, no need for alarm; there are plenty more ways to deal with …

CHAPTER 10

gripping stories

Did you ever get so absorbed in a book or article that you lost all track of time—you were so caught up in the content that you were hardly aware of the people or the room around you? Our mind is a master storyteller, and all it wants is our attention. Our mind tells us story after story, all day long. We commonly call those stories "thoughts." Some of these stories are indisputably true: we call them "facts." But the vast majority of the stories our mind tells us are not "facts"; most of them are opinions, judgments, beliefs, attitudes, ideas, assumptions, values, goals, expectations, wishes, fantasies, desires, attitudes, and so on. And as we get absorbed in those stories, we easily lose track of where we are and what we are doing. Ever been in a conversation with a friend, relative, or partner and suddenly realize you haven't heard a word they've been saying? Ever driven in your car and found that when you got to the destination, you couldn't remember the journey? Ever walked into a room to get something, but once there, you couldn't remember what it was? Ever been to a party or dinner or social event but been so caught up in your thoughts that you might as well not have been there?

These are just a few everyday examples of getting stuck inside-your-mind. But getting absorbed in stories is only one aspect of the problem; the other part is holding on to those stories. Worrying is a good example: your mind tells you a scary story about something bad your partner might do or something that might go wrong with your relationship. A common story is that your partner will leave you. Another is that you are trapped and you can't escape. Worrying simply means that you won't let go of these stories: you hold on to them and replay them over and over. Dwelling on the past—technically known as *ruminating*—is a similar process. You go over and over old hurts or painful memories; you replay them in your head and get yourself all worked up about whatever it was your partner said or did. And even though the past cannot be changed and dwelling on it serves no useful purpose, still you will not let go.

And aside from worrying and ruminating, there are all your judgments, criticisms, and rules of right and wrong; all your expectations, disappointments, and frustrations; all your fears of being abandoned, hurt, or controlled. Remember, though, these thoughts, beliefs, and memories do not create smog! The smog only happens when you hold on to them. As you loosen your grip, the smog disperses, freeing you up to explore the valley beyond.

learning to be flexible with your thoughts

Clench your hand into a fist. A tight one. Have a good look at it. Notice the shape, the contours, the white knuckles. While your hand is clenched tightly, what is it good for? Only one thing: aggression. You can use it to intimidate or deliver a blow, and that's about it. A clenched fist cannot gently stroke the face of a loved one, hold the tiny hand of a newborn baby, or softly caress the contours of your partner's body.

Now gradually release the tension in your fist. Open it up, uncurl your fingers, and let your hand relax. Now you can use your hand to write, paint, type, chop vegetables, drive a car, stroke a dog, brush your teeth, caress your partner's face, cradle your baby's head, or massage your aching temples.

When we hold on to our thoughts tightly, we become inflexible. Like a clenched fist, we are limited in what we can do. And when those thoughts are critical of our partner, we are likely to say or do something hurtful. But when we loosen the grip on those thoughts, when we hold them more lightly, we become more flexible and we can respond more effectively to our challenges.

techniques for tough thoughts

Learning to be flexible takes some practice. Here are some techniques that can help you:

exercise: *a fistful of thoughts*

To get the most out of this exercise, take your time as you move through each step. Read through the instructions once before beginning.

1. Bring to mind an unhelpful story about your partner. (*Remember:* When talking about "unhelpful," we're not talking in terms of "true" or "false" but in terms of "workable" or "unworkable." When we say a story is "unhelpful" or "unworkable," we mean that when you get caught up in it, your relationship suffers.)

2. Condense this story into a sentence or two.

3. For about twenty seconds, get all caught up in it—buy into it, fuse with it.

4. Hold your hand out in front of you, and imagine taking that story out of your head and placing it onto the open palm of your hand.

5. Slowly clench your fist as tightly as you can, gripping that story as if your life depended on it. Hold it tightly for a few seconds.

6. Slowly release your grip. Open up your hand and let the story rest there on your palm. Don't try to flick it away or wipe it off. Just let it sit there.

So what happened? Is that story still having the same impact on you? Or has it "lost its grip" on you? (Yes, gripping is a two-way street: you grip the story and the story grips you!) Hopefully you have experienced some defusion—a sense of stepping back from the thought and disentangling yourself to some degree. I encourage you to try using this technique whenever you realize you are holding on too tightly. If it doesn't do much for you, here are some alternatives:

exercise: *naming the story*

In the last chapter, we talked about the "bad partner" story. You can take this technique further: if you took every single unhelpful thought, feeling, and memory connected to your relationship issues and put them all into a book or a movie, what title would you give it? You can be as creative or as literal as you like: The Black Hole Story, The Big Mistake Story, The Lousy Marriage Story, or The Lazy Slob Story. For the next few weeks, as soon as you recognize any feeling, thought, or memory connected with this story, simply name it: "Aha. Here's The Life Sucks Story again!"

Of course, sometimes you will get hooked in by the story before you realize it. No problem. The moment you realize what has happened, just name it: "Aha! Just got hooked by The Nag Story again." Aim to do this with a sense of humor and playfulness; lighten up instead of being too serious about it. Over time, it should help you to hold the story more loosely and let it go more easily.

exercise: *singing the story*

1. Pick a nasty judgment or criticism of your partner and put it into a short sentence, no more than a few words long: "He's a selfish pig!"

2. Try singing it to the tune "Happy Birthday."

3. Try singing it to a tune of your choice.

What happened? Most people find the thought rapidly loses its power as they recognize it for what it is: nothing more or less than a string of words, just like the lyrics in a song. Those words, of course, may be true or false, exaggerated or realistic, harsh or fair, optimistic or pessimistic—but that's not the point! The point is simply this: they're just words. And once you can see the true nature of a thought—that it is simply a string of words (sometimes accompanied by pictures)—it is much easier to let it go.

exercise: *radio mind*

Imagine your mind is a radio. Listen to your thoughts as if you are listening to a sports commentator or news announcer. Notice where that voice seems to be located: is it in the direct center of your head or off to one side? Notice the speed and rhythm of the words. Notice the volume and the pitch. Notice the emotion present in the voice. Notice the pauses or gaps when the words stop or slow down.

Try doing this for five minutes initially. At times, you'll get so caught up in the content of the broadcast that you'll forget the point of the exercise. That's completely normal. As soon as you realize this has happened, take a step back and once again notice your mind as if it's a radio: notice the speed, volume, emotion, and delivery of the words rather than getting absorbed in the content.

exercise: *leaves on a stream*

This is a classic ACT exercise for learning how to let thoughts come and go. You'll need to set aside five minutes for it. Read the instructions through a couple of times, and then give it a try. (By the way, this is one of several useful exercises recorded on my CD *Mindfulness Skills*, volume 1. See Resources at back of book.)

1. Find a comfortable position.

2. Close your eyes or fix them on a spot, and take a few slow, deep breaths.

3. Imagine you're sitting by the side of a gently flowing stream. There are leaves floating on the surface of the water.

4. For the next five minutes, take every thought that pops into your head, place it on a leaf, and let it float on by. Alternatively, if you find visualization hard, just imagine a moving black strip or a moving expanse of blackness, and place each thought onto that. So if your mind says, *This is stupid*, you take those words, place them on a leaf, and let them float on by. And if your mind says, *This is boring*, you

take those words, place them on a leaf, and let them float on by. If your mind conjures up pictures rather than words, put each picture on a leaf, and let it float on by.

From time to time you'll get hooked in by a thought, and you'll lose track of the exercise. No problem. This is 100 percent normal, and you should expect it to happen again and again. This just gives you some insight into how easily your mind pulls you into its stories. As soon as you realize you've lost track of the exercise, start it up again.

If your thoughts stop, simply watch the stream or the blackness. Before long, your mind will start chattering again. If the same thought keeps popping up, no problem. Each time it does, just place it back onto a leaf.

Read the instructions again, then put the book down, and give the exercise a try for at least five minutes.

How did you do? This exercise, if practiced regularly, can really help you develop the skill of defusion. Five to ten minutes once or twice a day is ideal, but even a couple of times a week can make a difference. It's a great thing to do after you've just had a quarrel, when your partner has done something that annoyed or upset you, or indeed anytime you're feeling stressed or worried, or your mind is racing a million miles a minute. (If you predominantly hear your thoughts like a voice in your head and you find Leaves on a Stream rather difficult, then the Radio Mind Exercise may suit you better.)

LOVE and letting go

Remember the acronym LOVE from chapter 4? Notice how letting go, opening up, valuing, and engaging are all interconnected. When you let go of blame, judgment, and criticism, it is much easier to open up, act on your values, and engage in what you are doing. Letting go is a vital skill to develop; you will not be able to effectively discuss important issues, negotiate solutions, or reconcile your differences while you are in the grip of unhelpful stories. And you also can't move forward efficiently while you are desperately holding on to the past. So the more you can learn to hold these stories lightly and loosen your grip on those painful memories from the past, the more psychologically flexible you will become. Letting go is the key—and even taking a few seconds to clench and unclench your fist can act as a reminder.

At this point, you might be thinking, *Well, this is all well and good for dealing with my thoughts. But what about my feelings?* Ah, yes. Feelings. When your partner insults you or forgets about your anniversary, embarrasses you in public or says something hurtful that cuts you to the quick, stays out all night and comes home drunk, leaves clothes lying all over the house or promises to come home early but doesn't follow through, completely ignores you or makes an important decision without consulting you, or any other of a million and one things that push your buttons, at times like these, you need ...

CHAPTER 11

the kiss of life

Mouth-to-mouth resuscitation is such a dull term. In the old days, it was called "the kiss of life": you place your lips over someone else's mouth and breathe air into their empty, lifeless lungs. I think you'll agree, the old term is more poetic. The wondrous thing is you can give yourself the kiss of life whenever you need it. When the life is draining out of you, when you're suffocating in painful thoughts and feelings, then all you need to do is breathe mindfully. Open your mouth, breathe in some air, and draw it down into the very depths of your lungs. Appreciate it flowing in, much as you would a cold drink on a hot summer's day.

Mindfulness is about getting the most from life; it's about embracing each moment to the fullest and finding the richness within it. This involves a particular attitude: one of curiosity and openness. So mindful breathing means *really* noticing your breath, *really* paying attention, and genuinely being curious about it. When you breathe mindfully, you notice how your shoulders, chest, tummy, and nose all collaborate, acting in harmony to draw the air in and out of your lungs. Instead of taking it for granted, you appreciate your breath as the life-giving process that it is.

---

exercise: *breathing mindfully*

Breath as a life-giving process isn't something you can experience from reading a book; you need to actually practice it. So read through the following instructions a couple of times, then give the exercise a try. The aim in this exercise is to take ten slow, deep, mindful breaths. Focus on emptying your lungs completely, pushing every last bit of air out of them. This is important, as you can't take a deep breath in unless you first empty your lungs fully. Let's begin.

- Observe the breath flowing in and out of your lungs, as if you are a curious scientist who has never seen breathing before. Notice every aspect of your breath: the air flowing in through the nostrils, the rise and fall of your shoulders, the rise and fall of your rib cage.

- As you do this, your mind will tell you stories to try to distract you. Let those thoughts come and go, as if they are just cars driving by outside your house. Let your mind chatter away as if it is a radio playing in the background.

- If you get caught up in your thoughts and lose track of your breathing, that's normal. Expect this to happen repeatedly. When you're new to this exercise, you're doing well if you last ten seconds before you "drift off." So, as soon as you realize you're drifting off, take a moment to acknowledge it and then gently refocus on your breath.

- Observe your breathing as if it is the lead singer in a rock concert. The singer is the center of your attention, but you don't have to try to ignore all the other musicians and performers on the stage. Likewise, in focusing on your breath, you're not trying to ignore or blot out all your thoughts and feelings; you're not trying to get rid of them or "clear your mind." You remain aware of them, but your attention is firmly centered on your breathing.

- Now give it a try: mindfully take ten slow, deep breaths.

How did you do? Some people find this easy, whereas some find it very hard. Most people find it calming, but a few initially find it frustrating. However you found it, I hope you'll be willing to practice it, because if you do, you'll discover that this simple mindful breathing technique can easily become one of the most useful tools in your life. It is like dropping an anchor when you're in the midst of an emotional storm. It won't get rid of the storm, but it'll hold you steady until the storm passes.

dropping anchor with mindful breathing

I want to explain the previous paragraph in more detail. It's important to recognize that mindful breathing is not a relaxation technique. If you wish, you can turn it into one. If you practice it in a stress-free, nonchallenging environment, then it is likely to be very relaxing. But if you do it in the midst of a stressful situation, it will not relax you; in fact, nothing will. This is because your body has evolved over millions of years to have a "fight-or-flight response" whenever you are in a challenging or threatening situation. A *fight-or-flight response* means your body revs itself up to either run away or stay and fight: your heart races, muscles tense up, adrenaline levels rise, and you experience strong feelings such as fear or anger. No relaxation technique known to humankind can reverse this response while you're actually in a challenging situation. Evolution has hardwired you this way. If a huge deadly beast with gaping jaws full of razor-sharp teeth charges you, your brain wants you to either run as fast as you possibly can to escape it or to stand your ground and fight it off. Your brain definitely does *not* want you to lie down and relax. So relaxation techniques will not work while you're in a challenging or threatening situation.

Obviously once you remove yourself from that situation, it's a different story. If you've ever learned a relaxation technique, you'll recognize this from your own experience. The techniques work well when you're sitting in a park on your lunch break, listening to a CD in your bedroom, lying on the floor after a yoga class, or sitting on the couch in your therapist's office, but they do not relax you when you are in the midst of a genuinely challenging situation, such as giving a speech, taking an exam, going for an interview, or having a difficult discussion with your partner about a painful issue.

So mindful breathing is first and foremost an anchor. It holds you steady until the storm subsides, but it's not a magical method for calming the waves. This means you will get the best results if you regard it as a way of grounding and centering yourself, instead of treating it as a relaxation technique. (As I said, you *can* use it as the latter, but by far its greatest benefit is as the former.)

You can think of mindful breathing as a sort of playground slide: it allows you to slide from your mind down into your body. Once in your body, you're able to take control of your arms and legs, and use them for effective action. So mindful breathing serves two useful purposes: it gets you out of your mind, and holds you steady in the midst of painful feelings. When you're anxious, angry, resentful, worried, guilty, jealous, furious, or just plain hurting, it's amazing how useful a bit of mindful breathing can be.

There are at least three reasons why mindful breathing is so useful. First, slow deep breathing helps to settle down a revved-up nervous system. It is not some magical way to control your feelings, but it will help to lower your level of arousal and ground you in the present moment.

Second, the fact that you are breathing tells you something very important: that you're alive. This is good news. If you're alive, there is always something meaningful or purposeful that you can do. Third, mindful breathing gives you a few moments to get your act together. When your thoughts are spinning like a merry-go-round at full speed, mindful breathing helps you to step off the ride and give yourself a bit of "breathing space."

So make mindful breathing part of your daily routine. Whenever you're stressed, upset, angry, anxious, or lonely, take some slow, deep, mindful breaths, and center yourself. And there's nothing magical about the number ten; it could be three or five or seven. Even one slow, deep, mindful breath can be helpful; in the space of five or six seconds, you can slide out of your mind into your body and anchor yourself fully in the present moment. Why not practice this while at red traffic lights, in supermarket lines, and during the commercial breaks on TV? The more you introduce this into your daily routine, the more natural it will become. That means when you're in conflict with your partner and those strong feelings start surging through your body, you'll be able to drop an anchor and act effectively.

One more thing: if you're willing to practice, you can readily turn this simple technique into an intensive mindfulness training tool. You don't have to do this, of course. But if you're interested, and willing to work on it, then you can use the following guidelines.

---

exercise: *do-it-yourself mindfulness training*

This exercise will benefit you in at least three ways if you practice regularly:

1. It teaches you to focus and stay present. If you're like most people, you'll find it is very hard to stay focused on your breath; usually, within ten seconds or so, you'll get pulled back inside-your-mind. This exercise hones your ability to stay present, to catch yourself when you've "drifted off," and to then refocus. Imagine how useful it could be if instead of drifting into the smog and disconnecting from your partner, you could remain present and connected!

2. It teaches you to let go of unhelpful thoughts. Imagine if you could let go of all those unhelpful beliefs, judgments, and criticisms about your partner; if they had no more influence over you than a TV commercial for some useless product; if you could let them come and go without getting caught up in them or pushed around by them, how much easier would your life be? How much would your relationship improve?

3. It teaches you to stay centered and grounded, instead of getting swept away by strong feelings. It also teaches you to find a calm space inside you, even as your emotions churn through your body.

So what's involved? It's very simple. Instead of taking ten mindful breaths, you find a quiet place, sit comfortably, and practice your mindful breathing for five or ten or fifteen minutes. It's up to you. The longer you practice, the more you hone your mindfulness skills. Most people start with five to ten minutes once a day, then gradually over a few weeks, they build to ten to fifteen minutes twice a day. But every little bit counts; if you practice for only three minutes a week, that's better than not at all. (And if you'd like a voice to guide you through this practice, you can use my CD *Mindfulness Skills*, volume 1. See Resources at back of book.)

surely there must be more?

I know what you're thinking: there must be more to managing feelings than this. You're absolutely right! Emotions and feelings are complex, and there are many effective ways of responding to them. But mindful breathing is an incredibly useful tool to have in your kit. When the storm comes in, drop anchor. Once you are firmly anchored in the harbor, you can safely come out on deck and observe the elements. And from that position, instead of struggling with a feeling, you can ...

CHAPTER 12

name it and tame it

The great philosopher Jean-Paul Sartre once made this famous remark: "Hell is other people." He was only half-right. Heaven is other people too. In other words, our deepest relationships give rise to the most dreadful feelings and the most wondrous feelings. Alas, we don't get to have the "good" ones without the "bad" ones.

I've put "good" and "bad" in quotes because, believe it or not, there's really no such thing as a good or bad emotion. Describing them as good or bad is just the judgment machine at work again, setting you up for a struggle with your own normal feelings. Suppose you judge a job as "bad." What happens to your relationship with that job? And if you judge a person as "bad," what happens to your relationship with that person? And if you judge a feeling as "bad," what happens to your relationship with that feeling? When you judge your feelings as "bad," you struggle with them. And the more you struggle with them, the more intense they become. You get stressed about your stress, angry about your anger, or anxious about your anxiety. You may even feel guilty about your worry about your resentment!

To live a full human life means to feel the full range of human emotions. Therefore it's far more useful to talk of pleasant versus painful emotions rather than good or bad emotions. Now before reading on, take a few moments to think of the main problems in your relationship.

Really think hard about them—fuse with all your psychological smog—and after a minute or so, see if you can name some of the painful feelings connected with these issues.

our feelings—and how we deal with them

As you fused with your psychological smog, how many painful feelings did you experience? If we allow ourselves to get swept up and carried away by judgments and criticisms, we quickly descend into a dark, dank pit of contempt, anger, frustration, and resentment. If we get lost in doom-and-gloom thoughts, we rapidly fall into sadness, despair, frustration, disappointment, loneliness, and hopelessness. If we wander off into scary thoughts, we'll soon be stumbling around in anxiety, fear, insecurity, vulnerability, and worry. If we get hooked by hurtful memories, we are soon swamped in sadness, anger, hurt, distrust, resentment, revenge, jealousy, guilt, and shame. If we hold on to the "it's all too hard" story, we sink into helplessness, despair, meaninglessness, and apathy.

These feelings are all very common. They are exactly the emotions we expect normal, healthy human beings to have when things are going badly in their relationships. The greater the gap between what you want and what you've got, the more painful the feelings that will show up.

As your relationship improves and the tension and conflict decrease, those painful feelings will show up less often. However, you can guarantee that no matter how good it gets, there will always be areas of tension and times of conflict, which means that sooner or later those painful feelings will return. This is especially true if you have some of those deep-seated fears we mentioned in chapter 8: that your partner will abandon, control, or "smother" you.

So when those painful feelings show up, does it help you to wallow in them? Is it helpful to analyze them, dwell on them, or struggle with them? Is it helpful to let those feelings push you around and tell you what you can and can't do? The better you can handle your own feelings, the better you'll be able to handle those of your partner. Mindfulness helps you to do this. The starting point is to recognize that when we experience painful feelings, we commonly switch into one of two modes: avoidance or automatic pilot. Let's take a closer look at each.

Avoidance Mode

Avoidance mode means trying to do whatever you possibly can to avoid or get rid of unwanted feelings. Common examples of avoidance include distraction, opting out, thinking strategies, and substance use. Now let's take a quick look at each of these types of avoidance.

Distraction. You distract yourself from your feelings through TV, books, computer games, e-mail, Net surfing, socializing, gambling, exercise, working hard, and so on.

Opting out. You opt out of situations where unpleasant feelings arise. You may physically withdraw from your partner, go out of your way to avoid her, or avoid discussing important issues with him. And if physical or emotional intimacy brings up feelings of anxiety, insecurity, or vulnerability, then you may avoid being intimate.

Thinking strategies. You may try to deal with your feelings through a variety of different thinking strategies: trying to figure out why you're having these feelings, rehashing the past, beating yourself up, blaming your partner, telling yourself *I shouldn't be feeling this way*, analyzing your partner, debating with yourself, using positive affirmations, fantasizing about leaving, and so on.

Substances. You may try to push your feelings away by putting substances—such as cigarettes, alcohol, ice cream, chocolate, pizza, chips, prescription medications, recreational drugs, and others—into your body.

Many of these strategies give some short-term relief from your painful feelings, but it's rarely long-lasting. And you've probably noticed that the more intense your feelings, the less effective these strategies are; if you're feeling extremely anxious or furious or guilty, then eating chocolate or drinking beer or watching TV probably won't make you feel any better. Avoidance strategies are not usually problematic if you use them flexibly and moderately. But if you use them rigidly or excessively, they will soon drain your health, vitality, and well-being.

For example, if you overrely on distraction, you will end up wasting large amounts of time doing stuff that is not fulfilling or meaningful.

(Let's be honest: how many hours of your life have you wasted watching crappy television? Even something as innocuous as watching TV can destroy a relationship if you do it to such a degree that you neglect to invest time and energy in your partner.)

Similarly, if you do too much opting out, you may end up cut off, isolated, and alienated from your partner, which drains all the intimacy and openness from your relationship. If you overdo it with the thinking strategies, you're likely to waste huge amounts of time trapped inside-your-mind. And the more you rely on pumping substances into your body, the more likely you are to end up with health problems, ranging from weight gain to disease or addiction.

Thus the more you rely on avoidance to manage your feelings, the more your quality of life suffers. It's not that avoiding our feelings is inherently "bad." We all do it at times. It only becomes an issue if our avoidance is excessive or inappropriate. In other words, it's all about workability. If a given avoidance strategy does not harm you or your relationship, no problem. But if it's sucking the vitality from your relationship or holding you back from making important changes, then we would say it is "unworkable" and therefore it's wise to do something about it.

Automatic-Pilot Mode

Automatic-pilot mode means exactly what it says: when strong feelings show up, you allow them to push you around as if you are a robot with no conscious will. In this mode, you become the "reactive partner." You act out mindlessly or impulsively, with little awareness of what you're doing. For example, if anger shows up, you allow it to jerk you around like a puppet on a string, you yell or lash out, you say hurtful things, or you storm out of the room and slam the door. Or if jealousy shows up, you may fly off the handle without any justification, start spying on your partner, or make unfair accusations. Or if fear shows up, you allow it to command your every move: you may hide away, avoid taking risks, or run away from your challenges.

When you go through life in this mode, you often end up doing things you regret. You have little or no self-awareness, and tend to take action without much care or deliberation. As a result, you often act inconsistently with your own core values.

what are the alternatives?

The alternative modes to avoidance and automatic pilot are acceptance and awareness. In *acceptance mode*, rather than trying to get rid of our emotions, we learn how to open up and make room for them; we give them space so they can come and go of their own accord without getting in our way. Remember the acronym LOVE—letting go, opening up, valuing, engaging—that we talked about in chapter 4? Acceptance is the "opening up" component of LOVE. Opening up to your feelings doesn't mean you like them, want them, or approve of them—it simply means you allow them to be there; you make room for them; you don't waste your time and energy in fighting them, suppressing them, or running from them.

Awareness mode is pretty much self-explanatory: you are no longer on mindless, robotic automatic pilot. Instead you are fully conscious of your feelings and your actions. In terms of LOVE, you are "engaging": making full conscious contact with what is happening right here, right now. When you are fully aware of what is happening, both in the world around you and inside your own body, then you are able to take control of your arms and legs, and to act the way you truly want to. In awareness mode, no matter how strong your feelings are, they cannot control you. No longer are you a puppet on a string; no matter how challenging the situation is, you can now *choose* the way you are going to act.

Mindfulness is a mental state of both awareness and acceptance. In a state of mindfulness, you are conscious of your feelings and open to them. This means they have much less impact and influence over you, thereby freeing you up to act on your values and engage in what you are doing.

NAME your feelings

If you want to handle your feelings effectively, NAME them. NAME is an acronym for:

N – Notice

A – Acknowledge

M – Make space

E – Expand awareness

Let's go through these steps for handling your feelings, one by one.

Step 1: Notice

When strong feelings show up, the first step is simply to notice them. This is not always easy. In fact, the more intense your emotions, the harder it is. There are two main reasons for this.

First, by the time you reach adulthood, your habitual responses to your emotions are deeply entrenched. You have become an expert at living on automatic pilot; your natural tendency is not to notice what you're feeling until after you've already acted on it. It takes quite a bit of practice to unlearn these habits.

Second, when strong emotions arise, your mind tends to go into a frenzy. Your psychological smog gets all stirred up, growing thicker, darker, and stickier until soon you are completely lost. And the more fused you become, the less your capacity for awareness. Thus in order to work effectively with your emotions, you will first need to disperse the smog. That's where some mindful breathing comes in handy:

- First breathe out fully, pushing all the air from your lungs. Then allow them to fill from the bottom up.

- As you do this, notice your breath flowing in and flowing out. You can think of your breath as an escape chute: it helps you to slide from your mind into your body.

- You may find it helpful to say to yourself something like "Letting go," "Stepping back," or "Dropping the story"— or perhaps something humorous like "Bye-bye, smog" or

"See you later, mind." (It's not essential to do this, but many people find it aids defusion.)

- Next, move your awareness from your breath to your body, and notice where this feeling is most intense. We characteristically feel strong emotions in certain areas of our body: most commonly our forehead, jaws, neck, throat, shoulders, chest, or tummy. So check out your body. Take a few seconds to scan it from head to toe, and zero in on wherever the feeling is strongest.

- Notice where this feeling starts and stops. Where are its edges? Is it at the surface or deep inside you? Is it moving or still? What temperature is it? Does it have hot spots or cold spots? Notice as much about it as you can, as if you are a curious scientist who has never encountered anything like it before.

Step 2: Acknowledge

Once you've noticed the feelings and sensations in your body, the next step is to openly acknowledge their presence. This can be done with some simple self-talk. Say to yourself, "Here's a feeling of anger" or "Here's a feeling of insecurity." In ACT, we encourage you to describe your feelings in this manner rather than saying "I'm angry" or "I'm resentful." Why? Because when you say "I am guilty" or "I am sad," it seems as if you *are* your emotion, which makes it seem much larger than it actually is. In ACT, we want you to experience that you are *not* your emotions in the same way that you are *not* your thoughts. Thoughts and feelings come and go; they pass through you, much as clouds pass through the sky; they are transient events, continually changing. They are not you. Even the common phrase "I am feeling angry" could be better stated as "I am having the feeling of anger." Notice how the latter description helps you to step back from the feeling a little.

An even simpler option is to label your feeling with just one word: "anger," "guilt," "fear," "sadness." And if you can't quite identify the emotion, you can use a vague term like "pain," "hurt," or "stress."

Acknowledging is an important step in acceptance. It means you are "getting real"—that is, that you are opening up to the reality that this is what you are feeling in this moment. It's like skating on thin ice: if you want to deal effectively with the situation, the first step is to acknowledge that the ice is thin.

Note: It is important to acknowledge your feelings nonjudgmentally. If you say to yourself, "Here's this terrible feeling again!", that's likely to lead you to avoidance, not acceptance.

Step 3: Make Space

When painful feelings show up, we tend to tighten up around them. Rather than give them space, we try to squeeze them out or squash them down or push them away. This is like locking an angry or frightened horse inside a small tin shed. The horse will pound its hooves against the sides, hammering away, frantic to escape—and in the process, it will do a lot of damage. But suppose you release that horse into a large open field. There it can run around to its heart's content. Soon it will expend all its energy and settle down. No harm done. In much the same way, we can learn to open up around strong feelings. If we give them plenty of space, they will expend their energy without harming us. Your breathing can help you with this:

- Breathe in deeply. Imagine that your breath flows into and around that feeling in your body. And as it does, it's as if, in some magical sense, a space opens up inside you. It's a sense of opening up, of making room for all those unpleasant sensations.

- See if you can allow those feelings to be there, even though you don't want them. You don't have to like them or want them. You are simply giving them permission to be present.

- This is not a clever way to get rid of the feeling. It is merely a way to make peace with it—to stop fighting or running from it.

■ You may find it helpful to use some self-talk. Perhaps say to yourself, "Opening up," "Making space," or "Let it be." Or perhaps try a longer phrase: "I don't like it, I don't want it, but I can make room for it."

■ Keep breathing into and around your feelings. Open up little by little, making more and more room.

■ You can make this exercise as short or as long as you like. You can do a one-minute version or a twenty-minute version. With practice, you can run through the whole exercise in ten seconds, which is about the time span of one slow, deep breath.

Step 4: Expand Awareness

The final step is to expand awareness—in other words, reach out and make contact with the world around you. Life is like a magnificent ever-changing stage show, and on that stage is everything you can think, feel, see, hear, touch, taste, and smell. This feeling in your body is only one actor upon the stage. For a few moments there—in steps 1, 2, and 3—you dimmed the lights on the stage, and you shined a spotlight directly onto this feeling. Now it's time to bring up all the lights again. Notice the whole stage show; notice everything you can see, hear, touch, taste, and smell. Look around the room. Where are you, what are you doing, who are you with? What can you see, hear, and touch?

As you do this, your feelings are still present, but you have made room for them; they can hang around until they decide to leave. Meanwhile you are free to act, guided by your values. So expand awareness: reach out and connect with the world around you. Rather than turn inward and close down, turn outward and open up. Then let your values gently show you the way: ask yourself, "What would I like to do right now that's consistent with my values?" Don't wait until you "feel better"; if there's something meaningful or important you could be doing, then do it right now!

why bother with all this?

In any meaningful relationship where you spend a significant amount of time with the other person, painful feelings will arise. This applies to all relationships: with friends, family, children, and parents. If you spend enough time with another person, then sooner or later they will disappoint you, annoy you, fail to meet your needs, or do something that upsets, stresses, or worries you. You can't prevent this any more than you can prevent spring from following winter.

In whatever relationship you have, your feelings will change continually—from delightful to dreadful, from delicious to dire. But don't let this get you down. With practice, you can learn to make room for such feelings, to let them come and go, neither avoiding them nor letting them control you. This applies to any feeling whatsoever: from fear to fury, from sadness to loneliness. The more you practice these skills, the more both you and your partner will reap the benefits.

"But," I hear you protest, "I can't do all that in the middle of an argument." You're absolutely right. Initially you'll need to practice this skill in your own space and time. For example, practice doing a thirty-second or one-minute version of the NAME process between five to ten times each day, whenever you feel stressed, frustrated, anxious, angry, or tense.

And if you're at home, and you're feeling all worked up, then you can practice this in more depth. Here's what you do:

- Find a comfortable place, sit down, and practice the four steps of NAME: notice, acknowledge, make space, expand awareness.

- Observe what you are feeling with genuine openness and curiosity, as if you are a scientist studying some amazing miracle of nature.

- As you observe the feeling, keep breathing into it.

- From time to time, you'll drift off into your psychological smog. This is normal. As soon as you realize it, refocus on your breathing. Then slide down your breath, back into your body.

Depending on the situation, you might do this for five to fifteen minutes or so. To begin, five minutes is a good start. (This is yet another exercise recorded on *Mindfulness Skills*, volume 1. See Resources at back of book.)

Over time, with repeated practice, you *will* be able to do this in an argument. You'll be able to notice yourself getting worked up, and you'll be able to drop an anchor instead of getting carried away. Your partner will say something provocative or hostile, and a flood of feelings will surge through your body: hurt, anger, fear, frustration, or despair. But you will breathe into it, make room for it, and stay present.

Of course, there are bound to be times when you get so caught up in the conflict that you forget to do this. That's also a part of being human. If this happens, you can still practice the NAME technique. Practicing mindfulness *after* the argument is far healthier than going off and getting all caught up inside-your-mind, endlessly replaying the argument, and stewing on what your partner said and did.

what next?

So you've dropped an anchor, dispersed the smog, and made room for your feelings; what next? Well, next you tune into your values and use them to guide your actions. Hopefully you've already started doing this. And hopefully you'll now start doing more of it. Reflecting and acting on your values is an ongoing process: ideally you'll never stop until the day you die. On a daily basis, you can ask yourself, "What small actions can I take today to deepen and strengthen my relationship? What can I say or do that might make a difference?" Valuing could include anything from saying you're sorry to putting out the garbage, from buying flowers to making the bed, from sharing a funny story to snuggling up in bed, from offering to wash up to giving a massage, from asking "How was your day?" to saying "I love you."

So we've looked at letting go, opening up, and valuing. Now it's time to focus on engaging.

CHAPTER 13

look at me! look at me!

It's a sunny afternoon in the park. The little girl squeals excitedly as she cycles off down the hill. She lets go of the handlebars, lifts her arms high into the air. "Look at me! Look at me!" she yells. Her mother watches, smiling from ear to ear.

A young couple sits at a candlelit table. "You have amazing eyes," he says, holding her hand.

"Really?" she replies.

He nods, silently. As they gaze dreamily into each other's eyes, they are oblivious to everyone else in the restaurant.

the gift of full attention

One of the greatest compliments you can pay another human being is to give them your full attention. When you make someone the center of your attention, they feel important, cared about. They know they matter to you. And the reverse is also true. When someone is genuinely attentive to you, when you have engaged their interest, you feel pretty good, don't you?

Think of someone you greatly admire: your favorite movie star, athlete, author, rock star, or world leader—someone you'd love to meet in your wildest fantasies. Now suppose that person suddenly walked into the room. Would you give them your full attention? Absolutely! You'd "drink them in." You'd notice what they were wearing, how they were looking, what they were doing. And you'd listen with great interest when they were talking. You'd take note of their facial expressions, you'd register their tone of voice. You'd be keen to get their opinion, and you'd reflect carefully on whatever they had to say. And if they had some odd quirks to their personality, you probably wouldn't judge them harshly; you'd accept it as an oddity or eccentricity. You certainly wouldn't get upset about it or take it personally. And you'd probably feel some nerves or anxiety—as we often do in the presence of those we admire—but you'd make room for those feelings in order to spend some time with this person.

In this scenario, you are paying full attention; you are curious and open to the experience. In such moments, you experience a deep sense of connection; you are very much in touch with what is happening right here, right now instead of being lost inside-your-mind. This is what I mean by *engaging*.

In the early days of your relationship, you and your partner were both attentive to each other, curious about each other, and both very much "present." And then, over time, the magic wore off. Nothing abnormal about that—it happens to all of us. Here's why:

Your mind paints a portrait of your partner, and then mistakes that painting for the person. But a painting is static; it doesn't change. And after a while, you know every detail of that painting. Heck, you've seen it a million times and it's no masterpiece. So gradually you start to lose interest. You may still appreciate it, but it no longer captivates you. And so, bit by bit, the boredom creeps in. From time to time, you do stop to inspect it. But as time goes on, you seem to notice more and more flaws: the sloppy brushstrokes or the cracks appearing in the canvas. If you keep this up, eventually you will come to detest this painting and regret the day you ever set eyes on it.

Many relationships travel down this road: from fascination to boredom to contempt. But it doesn't have to be that way. If that's the road you're on, you can rapidly turn around through applying mindfulness: instead of focusing attention on your breath, you focus on your partner. You engage with him fully and completely. You notice her face, lips, eyes, posture, and actions. You notice the tone of his voice and the way he uses words. You are genuinely curious about her thoughts and feelings. You are intrigued by the way he sees the world. Your partner now becomes your anchor; when you drift off into your thoughts, you recognize it and pull yourself back to your partner.

Mindfulness helps you separate the person from the painting. You realize there's far more depth to this human being than any static portrait could ever capture. You realize the painting is a caricature: a few symbolic elements of this person, thrown together in a crude, cartoonish image. Look at the painting close up and you see it's nothing but a layer of paint on a bit of canvas. But look at the real person and discover just the opposite: there you'll find depth, life, and meaning.

The word "engage" is derived from two French words: *en*, which means "make," and *gage*, which means "pledge." When you engage fully with your partner, you are making a pledge—one of friendship, caring, and respect. At a level deeper than words, you are sending this message: *I respect you, I care about you, I am here for you.*

Engaging with your partner can be hard. Your mind will try to distract you. It'll throw you story after story, hoping one of them will grab you. And at times, it will succeed. But you can get better and better at letting go. You may also find painful feelings are an obstacle, especially resentment and anger. But you can get better and better at opening up and making room for those feelings.

Another potential obstacle is automatic pilot: going through the motions without tuning into what really matters. But you can get better at connecting with your heart and consciously acting on your values.

You can see, then, that these four elements of LOVE—letting go, opening up, valuing, engaging—are interconnected. They are four different facets of the same diamond: psychological flexibility. The *feelings* of love will come and go, but the *actions* of LOVE can be taken any time and any place, regardless of how you are feeling. And the more you do the actions of love, the more your relationship thrives.

there's more to engagement than a ring

We've talked a lot about engaging; now it's time to put it into practice. Here are a few suggestions for connecting mindfully with your partner. As you do each of them, let go of any judgments or criticisms—and if you realize your mind has carried you off, acknowledge it and gently refocus.

Be mindful of expression. Notice your partner's facial expressions: notice the lines and creases around her eyebrows, forehead, and mouth. See if you can trace her emotions. Watch as if you had paid a small fortune to witness the performance of a great actor: what is she expressing with her face?

Be mindful of body language. Notice how your partner moves his body: his neck and shoulders, arms and legs, hands and feet. Watch the way he gets into a car, climbs the stairs, or walks down the hallway, as if you'd never seen him do this before. Notice the gestures his hands make when he talks. Notice how his posture changes with his emotions. Watch as if you are a friendly anthropologist, observing a native of some long-lost civilization.

Be mindful of speech. Notice how your partner speaks: the rhythm and sound of her voice, the words she uses, the speed and tempo, the emotional overtones.

Be mindful of emotions. Practice all of the above simultaneously: notice your partner's face, body, and speech, all at once. Aim to tune into emotions; sense what your partner is feeling.

Cultivate curiosity and openness. When we talk, we like others to listen attentively. We like to know that they're interested and that they're open to hearing our thoughts and ideas, even if they don't agree with us. We don't feel good if the listener seems bored, distracted, hostile, critical, or dismissive. When interacting with your partner, you can cultivate curiosity and openness in several ways:

■ Ask questions that help you to see the world from your partner's point of view, such as, "How do you feel about that?" or "What do you make of that?"

■ When your partner speaks, listen as if your main aim is to make him feel important and cared about.

■ Listen with the intention to learn: to discover what your partner is feeling and thinking, to discover more about how she sees the world.

■ Listen with the intention to connect: to interact and bond at a level deeper than words, to let him know that you are there and that you care.

■ Let go of the unhelpful stories that your mind tells you. You know the ones: *Here we go again—same old story. You don't know what you're talking about. I wish you'd just sort this out, and that's the end of it. I know exactly what you're going to say. I can't be bothered with this.* You can't stop your mind from throwing up these sorts of thoughts, but you can let them come and go as if they're just cars passing by outside your house.

■ To help with all of these efforts, you might like to pretend you're on a first date: not only do you want to make a good impression, but you also want to know this person better. Ask questions and listen to her responses with the genuine intention of finding out more about her. Go on a voyage of discovery rather than assuming you already know him. *Remember:* the portrait is not the person. Take every opportunity to put the painting aside and meet the real human hidden behind it.

why bother?

Why bother with all this hard work, when it's so much easier to switch off, half-listen, change the subject, or put forward your own opinions and ideas without taking account of your partner's? The answer is because it's the antidote to boredom and disconnection. If you don't make the conscious effort to be curious, open, and attentive, you'll grow increasingly disinterested and dissatisfied with your partner—and vice versa.

---

if your partner is willing

These two exercises are powerful ways to enhance and develop your mindfulness skills. The first exercise is very challenging, and the second is less so.

exercise: *mindful eye-gazing*

This exercise is not for the faint of heart. Most couples find it's incredibly powerful; however, it can be unsettling for some people. One thing is for sure: don't attempt it unless you are both absolutely 100-percent willing to give it a try. If either partner feels coerced, this will backfire horribly. Generally five minutes is enough, but you can make it as short or as long as you like. Either partner can stop the exercise at any point by saying, "Okay. That's enough now." Read through the instructions and the comments on mindful eye-gazing once, then begin this simple exercise.

- Sit directly opposite each other, knees interlocking.

- For the next five minutes, gaze mindfully into each other's eyes *without talking*.

Your aim is to create a deep connection, to be fully present with each other. Don't turn it into a staring match! Your aim is purely and simply to deeply connect, to let this person know that he or she is the absolute center of your attention.

Uncomfortable feelings may arise. If so, breathe into them and make room for them. Your mind will try to distract you. Let your thoughts come and go like cars driving past your house, or leaves floating by on a stream. From time to time, you'll drift off into your mind. This is normal and inevitable. So as soon as you realize it, gently refocus. And if you start zoning out, zone back in. If you start laughing, don't try to stop it; let yourself laugh, but keep connected. Keep looking into your partner's eyes as you laugh. And the same goes if you shake or blush or cry.

Now read the instructions again, then give it a try.

Afterward discuss what happened. How did your mind try to distract you? What difficult feelings showed up? How hard is it to be truly present with another human being? Did either of you try to disrupt the exercise—by making silly faces or a silly noise? If so, what uncomfortable feelings were you trying to avoid?

exercise: *mindful cuddling*

This is a less challenging exercise. Follow the same instructions as for the last exercise, but this time, instead of staring into each other's eyes, cuddle up or hug for several minutes. Do this mindfully: cuddle as if you've never done it before. Notice where your bodies connect, and the feelings of warmth and pressure in those areas. Notice the rhythms of your breathing. Notice what you can feel underneath your fingers; notice what you can see, hear, and smell. Let your thoughts come and go, make room for your feelings, and focus your attention solely on the physical connection between you.

Afterward discuss what happened. How did your mind try to distract you? What difficult feelings showed up? Did either of you try to disrupt the exercise? If so, why?

The hippies were famous for their slogan, "Make love, not war!" It's a lovely ideal, but when it comes to intimate relationships, war is inevitable. However, if we bring LOVE to our battles, we can transform them. So without further ado, let's plunge into ...

CHAPTER 14

the heart of the battle

There are two types of couples in the world: those who fight, and those you don't know very well. Sometimes we meet a couple and they seem blissfully happy. They seem so well-suited; they have the same interests, desires, tastes, and fun-loving attitudes. And we think, "Wow! Why can't my relationship be like theirs?" We get sucked right back into the "perfect partner" story. We forget that all we've seen is a tiny glimpse of this couple; we've no idea what they're like behind closed doors. For all we know, they could be at each other's throats the moment they're home. We haven't a clue what they're like when they're sick or tired, or grumpy or bored or irritated. For all we know, they may yell, shout, and scream at each other all night long. But our mind conveniently forgets this. Instead it tells us that their relationship is wonderful, that's the way a healthy relationship should be, and there must be something wrong with ours because we fight so much.

learning to let go

Have you ever read about those fairy-tale marriages, the ones in the glossy magazines? Two rich, talented, sexy, beautiful movie stars get married, and they seem so happy and so well-suited and so in love. *A marriage made in heaven,* we think to ourselves. *They'll never fight and quarrel like we do, especially with all that wealth and luxury and glamour. What could they possibly fight about?* And then six months later, they divorce—and tell the whole world how awful their marriage was.

Now if you're prepared to completely straitjacket yourself, to suppress all your desires, put your life on hold, agree to your partner's every whim, and never protest or ask for what you want, then you may be able to get by without ever fighting. But what would be the cost to you and your life? To have a healthy relationship, you need to honor your values, goals, wants, and needs, as does your partner. And that is likely to lead, at times, to fighting. John Gottman, a giant in the field of human relationships, has studied hundreds of couples to discover the factors that make or break a relationship. His research clearly shows that what makes a relationship healthy is not the amount of fighting but the manner in which you do it (Gottman and Silver 1999). When fighting is mean and nasty—with volleys of harsh criticism and piercing insults amid a thick smokescreen of contempt and resentment—both partners get seriously wounded. But when the fighting is friendly—with some warmth, openness, and lightness, and without all that contempt, judgment, and resentment—then the wounds are only mild and heal very quickly.

This makes sense, doesn't it? You know what it's like when you have a light-hearted squabble with a close friend. You don't get deeply hurt or offended, and you get over it quickly. You also know what it's like when a quarrel "goes bad": when the daggers come out, and mean and nasty words get thrown around. When this happens, you *do* get hurt and offended—and then it's much harder to get over it. So how can ACT help us all to fight more fairly?

If you're lost in your psychological smog, you won't be able to discuss your issues effectively. You can't explore the valley when you can't even see it. However, if you can loosen your grip on all those unhelpful stories, you'll find your discussions are more constructive. Methods for letting go include naming your stories, identifying pet arguments, using humor, and revisiting the "I'm right, you're wrong" story. Let's look at each of these methods now.

Naming Your Stories

We talked in chapters 9 and 10 about naming your stories. You can apply the same approach to your recurrent arguments. First, identify the "classics": the ones you argue about over and over, year after year, without ever achieving anything useful. For most couples, this includes some of the following: finances, housework, holidays, domestic responsibilities, major purchases such as cars or houses, socializing, sex, raising kids, careers, work-life balance, and relationships with friends and relatives (especially in-laws). Pick one of your "classics" and consider: if it were a novel, what title would you give it? You can do this by yourself, but it's better if you can do it with your partner and have a sense of humor about it. Thereafter, when either of you notices the story, you can say, "Oops. Looks like we're getting caught up in The Housework Story." This can become a reminder to drop anchor: to breathe mindfully and stay present.

Identifying Pet Arguments

My wife, Carmel, dreamed this one up. One day we were talking about our "classic" arguments—keeping the house tidy, visiting relatives, spending money, and so on. We could rarely see eye-to-eye on these thorny issues. When it came to domestic cleanliness, she thought my standards were too low and I should work harder at keeping the house tidy and clean. In contrast, I thought her standards were too high and she created a lot of unnecessary extra housework.

Regarding visiting relatives, I thought she spent too much time with her family, and she thought I spent too little. With money, I thought she spent too much and too freely, and she thought I was too thrifty and too cautious. We had never made much headway on any of these issues, and we were starting to realize that we would probably never agree on them. Then Carmel said, "It's like they're our pet arguments. We keep them, and we feed them, and from time to time we take them out for some exercise." We both found this amusing. For all these years, we'd been trying to get rid of our pets! Poor little things! How rejected and unwanted they must have felt! Couldn't we give them a bit of affection for once?

When you look at your arguments as pets, suddenly they don't seem so big and troublesome. Your pets live with you, and you feed them, and you take care of them. The trick is to train them: lay down the ground rules so they don't get out of control and demolish your house. Many couples find it useful to play with this idea. If your recurrent arguments were animals, what sort would they be? What would they look like? (You can have different animals for different arguments, or they could all be the same species.) What names would you give them?

If your partner is willing, do this exercise together, and have some fun with it. Then play around with it. For example, when you recognize the tension building, you might comment, "Looks like the pets have escaped again." Carmel and I had a well-established habit of arguing during long car journeys. We now find this doesn't happen if one of us says at the start of the journey, "So are we going to take the pets with us?" or "Any particular pet you want to bring along?"

Using Humor

The key in fighting with LOVE is to lighten up: humor and light-heartedness can go a long way. Why not agree on some sort of humorous signal or word that either of you can use as a reminder to let go? For example, you might use the phrase "Lllllllllllletting goooooooooo!"— said in that voice a cartoon character uses when he falls off the edge of a cliff. Use your creativity. Any words, sounds, or gestures that you both agree on can serve this purpose. But you do have to both agree on it, otherwise one partner may use a phrase that upsets or irritates the other.

Revisiting the "I'm Right, You're Wrong" Story

We looked at this story briefly in chapter 7, but it's such a huge source of conflict, we need to revisit it. Out of all the gripping stories your mind tells you, chances are the "I'm right, you're wrong" story is one of the most compelling. Have you ever tried to have a discussion with someone absorbed in this story, someone who absolutely insisted that he or she were right? If so, what was it like? And what effect did it have on your relationship with that person?

"I'm right, you're wrong" shows up in a variety of different forms. With Michael, it takes the form of "We need to invest our money in stocks and bonds. I've done the research; I know what's worth investing in. This is what we're doing."

With Lisa, it manifests as "That's not how you hold the baby. No, don't give her the bottle that way. No, that's not the way to put on her diaper."

With Jim, it sounds like "You don't know what you're talking about. Let me handle this."

With Kirsty, it's "Why do you always have to shout at the kids like that? That's not acceptable."

There are many, many other versions of this story: "It's your fault." "You always do this." "You never do that!" "You're not listening." "Do it this way." "No, we're going to do it that way." "Don't tell me what to do."

The message is always the same: "I'm in the right, and you are not—so back off, shut up, or do what I say!" This is manifested in many ways: stubbornness, arrogance, righteousness, egotism, and contempt; insisting on your own way, refusing to compromise, making important decisions by yourself without letting your partner have any input. It is a surefire recipe for frustration, conflict, and tension. And typically this story is tied into a lot of unhelpful judgments: the "right" partner commonly sees himself as smarter, stronger, or superior in some way, and he often judges the "wrong" partner as lesser or inferior in some way. And how do you feel when you're the one who is seen as being "wrong"?

On the other hand, how does it feel when you're holding on to "I'm right"? Most of us, if we're honest, find it empowering. We tend to feel strong and righteous. Our body pulses with energy. We feel revved up, powerful, ready for a fight. But the problem is we channel all this power into building a wall—a huge thick wall that separates us from our partner. On our side of the wall, each brick is painted in bold letters: "I'm Right!" No wonder we feel so empowered. However, on our partner's side, the view is not so great: each brick is painted with "You're Wrong."

That wall does not allow closeness or connection. It does not enable teamwork or collaboration. It does not facilitate friendship, fun, or intimacy. If you want to build a healthy relationship, you will need to pull this wall down.

Luckily, with a bit of willingness, that's not too hard, because unlike real walls, these aren't built of bricks and mortar. They're simply made of attitudes, beliefs, and judgments. You remove the wall in exactly the same way you disperse the smog: you loosen your grip. When you let go of the bricks, the wall falls apart.

So begin by naming the story. You could go for the obvious: "Here's the 'I'm right, you're wrong' story showing up again." Or you could say to your partner, with a sense of humor, "Hmmm. Is it just me, or are we playing the right and wrong game here?" You could also come up with some playful names for it: The Leave It to Me Story, The Mr. Fixit Story, The Do It My Way Story. Again, this approach works best if you and your partner both agree on a name so you can use it with a sense of lightness without either of you taking offense.

The point of naming it is to help you both recognize it when it is present. By knowing it is there and knowing the likely outcome if you get caught up in this story, you have a better chance of defusing from it. And if your partner is not willing to play along, you can always use this technique on your own. You can say to yourself, *She's playing right and wrong again.*

An important reminder here: It's very important to practice this on yourself. We all get caught up in "I'm right, you're wrong." While it's easy to see it in your partner, it's often hard to recognize it in yourself. But look for it and you'll see it. It may show up as criticizing your partner behind her back, in making important decisions without consulting her, or mentally rehashing all the things she says or does that are "wrong." Once you realize it, you might acknowledge, "Uh-oh! Just got all caught up in that old story again." Then take a deep breath and let it go. Come back to the present moment. Notice where you are and what you're doing. Ask yourself, "Is there something more useful I can do right now instead of getting caught up in this story?"

Sometimes you'll name the story but find it's just not that easy to let go. Perhaps you've just ended an argument on a heated or painful note. Perhaps you're replaying an argument from last night, or last week, or last month. And perhaps there's so much hurt, resentment, or anger, it seems to feed the story and make it bigger. If so, ask yourself, "Would

I rather be right or be loving? Would I rather be right or build a relationship?" These questions can help jolt you back to reality.

Sometimes a zany defusion technique might help you. Try singing your thoughts, saying them in a silly voice, or imagining them written in chocolate frosting on top of a huge birthday cake. Alternatively, find a quiet spot and do the Leaves on a Stream Exercise from chapter 10. For several minutes, sit quietly and put each and every righteous, vengeful, resentful, arrogant, or self-satisfying thought onto a leaf and let it gently float away down the stream.

if your partner is willing

I like to give couples a small card that they keep somewhere convenient, such as a mantelpiece or a refrigerator door. On one side of the card, I write, I'M RIGHT, YOU'RE WRONG! On the other side, I write, *Can we let go of this story and do something useful?* The deal is that as soon as they recognize what is going on, either partner can give this card to the other. This technique can easily interrupt a battle and remind both partners to let go of the story. Try this for yourself, changing the words to suit your own style. You can even make several cards and leave them in different places.

the last word

One of the most useful things you can do in terms of ending an argument is to let go of the need to have the last word. If you won't let go, you can keep an argument raging on for hours, especially if you do the "You started it!" routine. I take it you know this one. It goes like this:

"This would never have started if you hadn't said ABC."

"No, you started it when you said DEF."

"But I only said that because you said GHI."

"But I said that because last week you didn't JKL."

This can go on all night long without getting you anywhere. Even if you *do* eventually agree on who started it (which is highly unlikely), what have you achieved that's useful and relationship-enhancing? It's simply another version of "I'm right, you're wrong." So ask yourself, for the sake of your relationship, are you willing to let go of the need to have the last word? Are you willing to let that urge come and go without acting on it? If you're at all like me, this is a big task; it's much easier said than done. But if you're willing to work at it—to step back and ask yourself, *What's more important here, being right or building a relationship?*—you'll find it saves you from wasting a lot of time and energy. You can then invest this energy in something more constructive, as you'll discover in the next chapter.

CHAPTER 15

take off the armor

"I'm sick of this. How many times do I have to tell you? Why don't you ever listen to me?"

How would you feel if someone started a conversation with you and that was their opening line? Hurt? Offended? Anxious? Angry? If you start off with hostility, antagonism, bitterness, or harsh judgments, then—unless your partner is a saint, guru, or Zen master—you are effectively setting the scene for a full-scale battle (or a hasty retreat by your partner).

learning to fight fairly

If you're going to address an issue, first think about the outcome you are looking for. If you want to waste your energy in a useless fight, you know what to do: put on your armor, pick up your sword, and charge. Leap into the fray, armed to the teeth with accusations, strong words, criticisms, judgments, and angry or plaintive demands. It's guaranteed to waste your time and DRAIN your relationship (see chapter 2). But if you want to deal with a difficult issue in a way that *enhances* your relationship, then you'll have to do the opposite. You'll have to put down your sword, take off your armor, and approach your partner with open arms.

Naturally, doing this won't be easy. You'll probably feel vulnerable. Our word "vulnerable" is derived from the Latin word *vulnus*, which means wound. Without your armor, you could be wounded. Thus you're likely to feel anxious or on edge, tense or uptight. You certainly won't feel comfortable. This is natural. After all, you're taking a risk here. You don't know how your partner will respond. He might attack. She might run away. He might be scornful. There's no guarantee that your partner will respond the way you want. This is the inconvenient truth. And this is where your "opening up" skills (see chapters 11 and 12) will come in handy: you can breathe into these feelings, make room for them, and use your breath to anchor you in the present.

Once again, it's all about focusing on what is in your control. You can't control how your partner will respond. And you can't stop yourself from feeling uncomfortable. But you *can* make space for those feelings. And you *can* control what you say, when you say it, and how you say it.

What You Say

First think about what you want to achieve. Do you want yet another quarrel, or do you want to build and strengthen your relationship? If the latter, then what sort of words would be most effective? For example, if you were addressing this issue with your best friend or with someone you really admired and looked up to, what would you say to that person? How would you phrase it?

Another thing to consider: do you wish to make a threat, issue an ultimatum, deliver a command, or boss your partner around—or do you wish to make a friendly request? Threats, ultimatums, commands, and bossiness are likely to provoke a strong negative reaction. Not surprising really—after all, do you like people threatening you or issuing ultimatums? How do you feel when someone demands, insists, or tries to order you around? If you want any chance of reaching a friendly agreement with your partner, one that may get your needs met without damaging the relationship, then you'll need to make friendly requests. Treat your partner as a friend from whom you are asking a favor. Ask politely and warmly for what you want. And express gratitude when you receive it rather than taking it for granted. Of course your mind may say, *I shouldn't have to ask! He should just do it,* or *If I start doing this, she'll think I'm weak.* So come back to workability: if you get caught up in those thoughts and allow them to dictate what you do, will that help your relationship in the long run?

When You Say It

If you're going to address a difficult or challenging issue, it makes sense to pick your time wisely. When is your partner most likely to respond well? When is he least likely to respond well? Bad times to have these discussions might be when either one of you is tired, irritable, drunk, or having a bad day, or when the kids are acting up, the in-laws are over, or you're both stressed to the max. Better times are likely to be when you're both rested and the environment is not too stressful.

Now it's time for a reality check. Many couples don't feel like discussing their important issues when they're in a good mood. This is partly because when you're in a good mood, your problems seem smaller and easier to deal with. Also, you may think, *We're having a good day. Why spoil it?* In contrast, when you're in a bad mood, your problems seem bigger and you're more likely to be irritable or frustrated, and therefore you're far more likely to want to talk about them. So while it's easy to give the advice in this section, it's not so easy to apply it in real life.

Still, it's worth keeping in mind. The message here is be realistic, while applying this strategy as best you can. You may find it helpful to give your partner advance warning: "I'd like to discuss our finances with you. Can we make time for it one night this week?" You may also find it useful to step out of your usual environment: for example, go for a walk in the park or discuss it over a drink or coffee in a café.

How You Say It

While the words you use are important, so is the attitude with which you deliver them. If your voice is loud or hostile, if your facial expression is arrogant or contemptuous, if your body posture communicates resentment or frustration, then no matter how beautiful and poetic your words are, they will not be received well. I make this point to couples with a little exercise. I ask them to take turns telling each other, "You are wonderful," but they have to say it with a sneer on their face and a voice dripping with sarcasm. Then I ask, "Which had the most impact on you: the words or the attitude?"

So base your attitude on your values. What sort of partner would you like to be? Caring, compassionate, accepting, open, understanding, respectful, loving, and so on? Or bitter, hostile, disrespectful, contemptuous, cynical, resentful, and the like? See if you can cultivate your preferred attitude *before* you talk to your partner.

Here are some suggestions for how to do this:

- Reflect on what your partner does that you appreciate.

- Think about your partner's strengths.

- Bring to mind a fond, loving memory that involves both of you.

- Remember that you are both hurting. Think about previous fights and recall the things you've said or done that were hurtful. Use this to cultivate compassion. Tap into your natural kindness and see if you can spare a little for your partner.

- Tune into your core values. Ask yourself, *What do I want to stand for here? If this interaction was videoed, and broadcast on national TV, how would I like to come across? What qualities would I like viewers to see in me?* Make a commitment to let these values guide you.

stop the dirty fighting

Ask yourself sincerely what sort of partner you want to be. Do you want to win an argument at any cost, no matter how much damage you do? Is winning an argument more important to you than building a healthy relationship? What does it cost you to use nasty, sneaky, or mindless fighting tactics? Sure, you may win an argument, but is it worth it? Does it make you feel good about yourself? What does dirty fighting cost your relationship? And if you're wondering what I mean by "dirty fighting," here are some examples:

Springing the Ambush: Your partner has done something that you don't like but rather than address it, you hold on to it— sometimes for days or weeks. Then, in the heat of some conflict, you unleash it on her, like pulling a concealed dagger from your sleeve.

Ganging Up: You get a third party involved in the fight: a parent or your best friend. The two of you then gang up on your partner.

Punching Below the Belt: In the heat of the battle, you're hurting. You may not even realize it. You may have pushed your pain down, deep inside—hidden it under a seething mass of anger. And now, hurt and angry, you want revenge. So you decide to hurt your partner even more than she's hurt you. And out comes the secret weapon. You know exactly what to say to play on all her deep-seated fears and insecurities. If her deepest fear is that you'll leave her, this is when you threaten divorce. If he's been feeling sexually inadequate, this is when you tell him he's lousy in bed. Ouch! Ouch! Ouch!

Playing the Lawyer: This is a favorite tactic of people with good language skills or those who are very adept at debating. You twist your partner's words around, take them out of context, or exaggerate them to the point of ridicule.

Exhuming the Corpse: This is when you dig up that rotting old corpse. Your partner did something a long time ago that hurt you badly. Although it's already long since dead and buried, you just won't allow it to rest in peace. Whenever you need some extra ammunition, you dig up the corpse and throw it in her face: "See? See what you did?" It's a powerful tactic: guaranteed to open up old wounds and get you bogged down even deeper in conflict.

Doing the Silverback: Ever seen a silverback gorilla defend its territory: roaring loudly, beating its chest, baring its fangs? Some humans do this too, often accompanied by throwing objects or slamming doors. This sort of behavior is threatening to your partner—even if he is bigger and stronger than you—and extremely damaging to any sense of trust or security.

Name Your Own Tactics: Why not come up with some names for your own favorite tactics? (You can do this with your partner, if she's willing.) Notice which tactics you both use, and which you prefer to use. One thing you'll notice: all these tactics are designed to win the argument or inflict pain; there's no consideration or kindness for your partner. Imagine what would happen if you could tune into your values around caring and connection while you address important issues with your partner—how might things go differently? Recognizing and acknowledging the destructiveness of your tactics is the first step in changing them. But it's important to look at your own tactics first—before you look at your partner's—because that's where you have the most control. As you change your own tactics, you may well find your partner changes his too. If he doesn't, you can address the issue, but you can do so guided by your values instead of being pushed around by anger or resentment.

battle tactics: fight or flight?

When conflict breaks out with your partner, your fight-or-flight response instantly kicks in. This is a result of evolution. When your primitive ancestors encountered a hungry bear, they had only two choices: (1) run away very fast or (2) counterattack and fend it off or kill it. In other words, fight or flight. As a quarrel heats up, you may find flight mode predominates: you want to back off, stop the argument, leave the room, get away. If your partner follows or tries to stop you from leaving, your desire to run will get stronger. You'll feel under attack and trapped until eventually you reach a point where you feel like exploding. At that point, you may switch into fight mode and start lashing out physically or verbally. Or you may stay in flight mode, but rather than physically running away, you do so psychologically: you shut down, go quiet, say nothing, look away, or refuse to engage.

On the other hand, if you switch into fight mode, you're likely to want to chase after your partner, continue the argument, and keep going until you've won or made your point. If your partner withdraws or goes silent, you're likely to feel angrier and angrier. And if you go on automatic pilot and allow your emotions to run you, then you're likely to become increasingly provocative and hostile. You might even chase after your partner, following her around the house as she tries to get away. Of course you may also chase after your partner in flight mode, motivated by fear of abandonment: you're afraid he's going to leave you, so you follow him hoping to end the argument and reach a peaceful settlement.

So if you go on automatic pilot and let these primitive responses jerk you around, you can easily get caught up in prolonged quarrels and fights. Alternatively, vicious cycles can arise where one partner runs away and the other one chases, and both get more and more worked up. So take a look at your battle maneuvers: who runs and who chases? Take a look at the role you play in this cycle, and see if it's in accordance with your values. Is chasing after your partner when she is clearly trying to escape consistent with your values about caring, respect, and kindness? Is running away from your partner consistent with your values around connecting, collaborating, and assertiveness?

Notice there are no simple answers here. It's not that one partner is "right" and the other is "wrong." It's not that you "should" stop running away or stop chasing. It's about finding a balance that works for your relationship. And that will be different for every couple. Typically to break these cycles, the runner needs to run less and the chaser needs to chase less. It's much easier to make that happen if both partners agree to practice LOVE. Ideally you would both let go of the story, open up and make room for your feelings, tune into your values, and engage fully.

---

if your partner is willing

These exercises all involve talking openly and honestly. When you are talking, make sure you do so with warmth and openness. You're talking not to score points but to deepen your bonds. And when your partner is talking, listen mindfully. Don't interrupt him with smart comments. Listen as if your partner is a personal hero: someone you admire, someone whose thoughts you feel privileged to hear. (If your mind says, *Yeah right!*—then let that thought go. If you hold on to it, you know where that leads.) Practice engaging with your partner: notice her voice, face, and body language.

exercise: *fighting tactics you use*

Discuss the tactics you both use in fighting. Each start by acknowledging your own tactics: "When I want to win a fight with you, this is what I do ..." It's a good idea to write these down as you discuss them—in your journal or on the worksheet—so you can refer to them later. As a bonus, you might like to invent some playful names for these tactics. Once you have each listed your own tactics, then you can invite your partner to add any others. Say something like, "Okay, I've listed every tactic I can think of that I use. Can you think of any others?" Keep a sense of humor, even if you don't like what your partner says. Don't get defensive: "Bullshit, I never do that!" or "I haven't done that for years." Instead try, "Wow! I don't recall doing that one" or "Ah, yes. I remember vaguely doing that one. Seems like a long time ago."

exercise: *preferred tactics and ground rules*

Discuss your preferred tactics: in the ideal world, what would be your ground rules? Each partner should complete the following four sentences. When we're having a fight ...

- I'd like you to accept me doing this:

- I want to stop myself from doing this:

- I'm willing to accept you doing this:

- I want you to stop doing this:

exercise: *chasing and running*

Discuss chasing and running. Use it as an opportunity to understand your partner and to develop more compassion. Even if it doesn't come naturally, it's important to let your partner know your feelings.

Runners: How do you feel immediately before you run? Why do you run? How do you feel if he chases you?

Chasers: How do you feel if she runs away? Why do you pursue? How do you feel when you're chasing?

Put yourself in your partner's shoes. Think hard about what that would feel like. Tell your partner, as best as you can, what you imagine it must be like for him or her. See how accurately you can guess.

---

the choice is yours

Life isn't always ideal, and your partner may not be willing to cooperate. He may ridicule your attempts to change or stubbornly refuse to try doing anything differently. Naturally, if this happens, you will feel frustrated and disappointed. And yet ... all is not lost. After all, you still have control over what you do. Psychological flexibility gives you freedom. When you are fully present, open to your experience, defused from unhelpful thoughts, and connected with your values, you are free to make a choice. Will you choose to do the same old thing you usually do, or will you do something more workable? There is no "right" or "wrong" here, no "good" or "bad." There is simply a choice to be made. Will you run away, or stay and talk? Will you pursue, or let her go?

Whatever choice you make, pay attention to the results and notice what happens. If it turns out to be workable, then keep doing it. If not, have a look at what you can do differently, guided by LOVE. After every battle, consider:

- What stories did you get caught up in? Would you consider letting go of them?

- What feelings were problematic? Could you practice opening up and making room for them?

- What did you say or do that worsened the situation? What values-guided actions might be more effective next time around?

- Did you go on automatic pilot or get trapped inside-your-mind? How could you engage more fully next time this happens? What could you do to stay grounded, focused, and present?

no guarantees

An attitude of LOVE will almost certainly improve the outcomes of your arguments and reduce the damage done during the conflict. But it's important to be realistic here. The fact is sometimes your partner will respond the way you want, and sometimes she won't. Sometimes you'll both see eye-to-eye on an issue, and sometimes you won't. Sometimes you'll reconcile your differences with a win-win outcome, and sometimes you won't. When things go the way you want, you'll feel good. And when they don't, you'll feel pretty lousy. Are you willing to make room for all of this? If not, you're going to struggle with reality. And that's a fight that reality always wins!

CHAPTER 16

the power of asking nicely

Imagine you are the ruler of the world. You have absolute power over your partner. He or she has to obey your every command, no matter what. If this were the case, would you ever ask him nicely to do what you want? Or would you just tell him what to do?

If you cared nothing about the quality of your relationship, if her feelings meant absolutely nothing to you, if you simply didn't care whether she liked you or not, then you probably wouldn't bother asking nicely. There'd be no point.

But if you did care about his feelings, and you did care whether he liked you or not, that would change matters, wouldn't it? Then you might very well ask nicely, even though there would be no need to do so.

The thing is, you're not the ruler of the world, and you don't have absolute power over your partner. But … you do have the power to choose how you speak to others. You don't *have to* ask nicely for anything. But if you care about her feelings, and whether she likes you or not, then you'd be wise to consider doing so.

check your experience

Don't believe me; check your experience. Take a look at what happens when you start acting like a dictator: when you insist, demand, or order your partner around; when you shout, yell, or snap; when you get on your high horse and tell her what to do. Does she like it? If you take this tack with your partner, she will generally either resist, attack, or run away. And if she does comply, she will do so with resentment. And the same goes for pleading, threatening, whining, or sulking.

It's not that any of these strategies is "wrong" or "bad"; it's just that they're not workable. One of the most basic principles for getting your needs met is this: ask nicely. By "ask nicely" I don't mean beg or plead; I simply mean ask politely. You have a right to ask for what you want. Your partner has a right to be spoken to politely. So make your request a friendly one: without demands, threats, abuse, or insults. Many people find this hard to do because they won't let go of stories such as these:

"I shouldn't have to ask. He should just do it."

"I've tried asking nicely. She never listens."

"Why should I have to ask nicely? He doesn't deserve it."

"If I ask nicely, she'll ignore me. She only ever agrees when I get angry."

Are you willing to let these stories go? These thoughts may be partly true—or even totally true—but how does it work if you hold on to them tightly? Regardless of what has happened in the past, the fact remains: the best chance of getting your needs met *and* also building a healthy long-term relationship is to ask nicely. There are many ways to do this. For example, you could start off with a compliment, an expression of appreciation, or both: "Honey, I really appreciate the efforts you've been making to tidy up after yourself. I know it doesn't come naturally to you, but it makes my life so much easier." Next, when you make your request, you can use phrases such as, "I'd be very grateful if ..." or "I'd like it if ..." or "I'd really appreciate it if ..." or "It would mean a lot to me if ..."

Here's what happened when I suggested this to Sarah:

Sarah: But I'd be lying. I don't feel grateful if Steve puts the kids to bed. He's just doing what he ought to do. Why should I be grateful for that?

Russ: It sounds like you're holding on tightly.

Sarah: To what?

Russ: To the "Steve should do what I want" story.

Sarah: *(aghast)* Are you saying he should be allowed to do what he wants? Have a beer, sit in front of the TV, and leave it all up to me?

Russ: Not at all. Think about it this way. If you want Steve to put the kids to bed *and* you also want to build a better relationship, then what's going to work best—showing gratitude when he does what you want or taking the attitude of "About time you pulled your weight, Mister!"?

Sarah: But I shouldn't have to ask him. He should just do it.

Russ: Sarah, there are millions of people on this planet who would totally agree with you. This is not a question of right or wrong, true or false. It's a question of workability. The question is: if you hold that belief too tightly, and allow it to dictate the way you talk to Steve, then will it work to make your relationship better?

Sarah: *(reluctantly, sighing)* No.

It's very hard to let go of our "shoulds," but we need to hold them lightly if we want our relationship to thrive. So notice these stories when they show up, and let them come and go without getting caught up in them. And then do what actually works rather than what your mind says *should* work.

But what if you ask and she says no? Or he just ignores you? Or she pokes fun at you? Or he says yes but doesn't follow through? Naturally you'll feel annoyed or disappointed, and your mind will start telling you all sorts of unhelpful stories. This is where the challenge really lies. In these situations, can you practice LOVE—letting go of unhelpful thoughts, opening up and making room for your feelings, acting on your values, and engaging mindfully? If so, you are in a good position. By being psychologically flexible, there are many options open to you:

- You can persist in calmly and respectfully asking for what you want.

- You can explain how important this is to you and what it means to you.

- You can negotiate and aim for a win-win solution that meets both your needs.

- You can make some sort of deal: "You do this for me and I'll do something else for you."

- You can reach a compromise. (Compromises are usually unsatisfying for both parties, but they're a lot better than all-out warfare.)

- You can calmly and respectfully tell your partner how you feel about the situation: that you're annoyed, disappointed, sad, or frustrated. For example, you could say, "I am feeling very annoyed; you said you'd wash the dishes and you haven't followed through." (However, be warned: if you start yelling or snapping or throwing insults, it will only end in a quarrel. "Calm and respectful" wins the day.)

- You can accept that this is how it is for now, let it go, and address it again later if it still seems important.

These strategies are only likely to work if you remain open and receptive to your partner, and treat her with respect. Mindfulness is essential here; if you don't drop anchor and stay present, you are likely to say or do something self-defeating. If you fuse with unhelpful stories or get swept away by strong emotions, you're likely to start shouting, judging, criticizing, pleading, whining, making threats, or treating your partner with contempt. And you know where that leads.

Of course, these suggestions are by no means all your options. They are simply some of the more commonly used ones. The point is to remain mindful and let your values guide you. That way you'll be able to try out various approaches, notice the results, and over time discover what works best.

you can answer nicely too!

If your partner asks nicely for what he wants, it's only reasonable to reply in a similar fashion. Even if you don't like the request, there's no need to snap, grumble, or attack. You can say no politely and respectfully. But if you do agree to your partner's request, do so willingly. If you go along with it grudgingly or resentfully, that will only lead to friction and tension in the long run. When you do something to "get her off my back" or "stop his nagging," it's deeply unsatisfying. It's far more rewarding to do it as an act of love, guided by your values around caring and contribution. Think about how this action will help your partner, how it contributes to her health, happiness, and vitality. Then choose to do it willingly as an act of caring, even if it's a royal pain in the ass. If you do, you're bound to find it far more fulfilling than going through the motions with gritted teeth. But don't believe this just because I say so; check it out and trust your own experience.

furry friends and fierce fish

When it comes to your closest relationships, are you more like a puppy dog or a shark? This question comes from Tony Wallace, a group counselor in Canberra, Australia; he uses this question to help his clients clarify their attitudes. Let's consider this for a moment: what is a relationship like with a puppy dog? That little dog only cares about one thing: you! It just wants to be with you and to please you. The moment you come through the door, it's ecstatic to see you: jumping up, wagging its tail, trying to lick you. It never gets bored with you and never turns nasty. And it's always disappointed when you have to leave. You can ignore it, starve it, beat it—and still it just wants to be with you, to "love you" and please you. The puppy dog pays little or no attention to its own needs; it's all about giving!

Now what's it like to have a relationship with a shark? Pretty difficult. The shark doesn't care about you one bit. All it's interested in is its own needs—namely food. If you feed it well, it may leave you alone. But if you don't feed it, you're breakfast. Try to bond with a shark and you're wasting your time.

In a healthy human relationship, we need to find a balance between these two extremes. If the relationship is all about you—your needs, your wants, your desires—your partner will see you as a shark: he's always providing food to stop you from eating him, but he's getting nothing back from you in return. On the other hand, if your relationship is all about pleasing him, and you constantly neglect your own needs, then you will start to feel like a helpless puppy dog—and he will start to look like a great white shark.

It's rare that one partner is all shark and the other is all puppy dog; we've all got aspects of both these creatures inside us. But most of us would benefit from finding a better balance: to become a compassionate, caring human being who is respectful of *both* our own needs *and* those of our partner.

Are there areas of your relationship where you are a bit too shark-like? You may get your needs met in the short term, but what long-term effect does this have on your relationship? Do you care about your partner's feelings and whether she likes you or not? If so, what "shoulds" would you be willing to let go of? And what would you be willing to accept? To step out of shark mode, you need to tune into your values around caring, giving, kindness, support, equality, and respect for your partner. That doesn't mean turn into a puppy dog. It simply means that you actively invest in your partner's health, growth, and well-being as well as investing in your own.

Now in what areas of your relationship do you play the puppy dog? And what is this costing you in the long run? The puppy-dog role may give you some short-term benefits. It may help you avoid fears of rejection, abandonment, or being hurt. It may help you avoid anxiety around conflict. But it costs you heavily in terms of health and vitality. It leads you to feel burned-out, downtrodden, resentful, or drained. To step out of puppy-dog mode, you need to tune into your values around respecting yourself, nurturing yourself, being true to yourself, and taking care of yourself. That doesn't mean that you have to turn into a shark. It simply means you look after your own health and happiness as well as that of your partner.

if your partner is willing

The exercises that follow are designed to help both you and your partner get better at asking for what you want.

exercise: *learning to ask*

In turn, each of you describe how you would like your partner to ask for things. What sorts of words, gestures, facial expressions, and tone of voice would make you more likely to say (a) yes and (b) no?

exercise: *the cost of your behaviors*

Have a discussion about what behaviors you consider sharklike or puppylike. However, the aim is to identify and discuss *your own* behaviors, not your partner's. Talk about what this is costing you in the long run. Then it is your partner's turn to do the same.

While your partner talks, listen mindfully with openness and curiosity. Don't interrupt him or throw in your two cents' worth. Don't get defensive or critical. Don't start arguing or disagreeing. Regard this as an opportunity to learn about your partner's world and how he sees himself.

As an extra step—but only if you're both completely willing—invite your partner to give you some feedback: Does your partner agree or disagree with your self-assessments? Be careful with this. If you're not mindful, it can quickly turn into an argument.

LOVE is all you need—or is it?

The Beatles had a huge hit with their song "All You Need Is Love." And it's a beautiful theory, but how realistic is it? Well, it depends on how you look at it. LOVE—letting go, opening up, valuing, and engaging—is first and foremost about cultivating an attitude of psychological flexibility. The more you can make room for uncomfortable feelings, let go of unhelpful thoughts, stay psychologically present, and act in line with your values, the healthier a relationship you can build. However, in itself, psychological flexibility may not be enough. You may have to learn some new skills around communication, negotiation, problem solving, assertiveness, conflict resolution, or even anger management. These topics are beyond the scope of this book, but I can highly recommend the book *Couple Skills* by Matthew McKay, Patrick Fanning, and Kim Paleg (see Resources and Recommended Reading). It's a simple step-by-step guide to the skills most commonly taught in relationship counseling. And if you learn and use new skills in the service of your values, then that very process is, in itself, "valuing." In which case we could say, "Yes! LOVE *is* all you need!" But what you need and what you get are two different things. And we often find it very hard to accept that ...

CHAPTER 17

you can't always get
what you want

What is it you want most from your partner? Affection, understanding, intimacy, respect, approval? More sex, more support, more help, more social life, more family time? Do you want him to open up and share his feelings, listen more attentively, ask you about your day? Do you want her to chill out, go easy on you, initiate sex more often?

Whatever you want, here's a fact: either you will get it or you won't. As your relationship improves, you practice LOVE, and you remember to ask nicely for what you want, the chances are you will get your needs met more often. But that will not alter this basic fact of life: you can't always get what you want.

dealing with feelings: some strategies to use

The larger the gap is between what you want and what you've got, the more it hurts. For smaller gaps, you may feel disappointment, frustration, anxiety, insecurity, or rejection. For larger gaps, you may feel anger, resentment, jealousy, sadness, or regret. For massive gaps, you may feel rage, anguish, despair, or panic.

You can't stop these feelings from showing up. They are normal human reactions. But if you stay on automatic pilot when they arise, you will act in all sorts of self-defeating ways. So when these feelings do show up, drop an anchor, and then use one or more of these strategies:

■ Get present, breathe deeply, and slide out of your mind and into your body.

■ Name the feeling, open up, and make room for it.

■ Notice what your mind is telling you and name the story.

■ Push your feet into the floor, take a good look around you, and notice where you are and what you are doing.

■ Talk yourself through it: "I'm so angry right now. But I can make room for it. Breathe. Stay present. I can't control how I feel, but I can control how I act. What do I want to stand for here?"

There's one thing to be wary of here: your mind can make this gap much bigger than it needs to be. For example, it may tell you that you shouldn't have to ask for these things, or it shouldn't be so hard, or other people's partners aren't as selfish as yours, or if he really loved you, he'd do whatever you want. Disappointment and frustration are pretty much inevitable when your needs and desires aren't met. But if you're experiencing rage, despair, panic, or anguish, then such intense feelings are often signs that you're snared in an unhelpful story. If that's the case, you know what to do. Take a step back and notice what your mind is telling you. Acknowledge there's a gap, and at the same time, check to see if your mind is making it bigger. What unhelpful story is your mind telling you? Can you name that story and let it go?

Mindfulness doesn't get rid of the gap; it just helps you change the way you respond. Fusion pulls you into the gap and leaves you stuck there, trapped and squashed beneath all your thoughts and feelings. Mindfulness allows you to step out of the gap, to acknowledge it, and make room for it. Inside the gap, you're stuck; outside the gap, you're

free to move. So practice letting go and opening up. Then ask yourself
these questions:

- Is there some other way to meet this need?

- If my partner is unable or unwilling, how can I satisfy this
  need myself?

- Can I meet these needs through other relationships with
  my family and friends?

Strategies in Action: Alice and Jim

Alice wants more stimulating conversation from Jim. But Jim isn't
much of a talker at the best of times. His conversational skills are
nowhere near as developed as hers, and his main interests are politics
and sports, neither of which interests her. After years of judging and
criticizing him, after countless hours spent dwelling on how her life
would have been better with someone else, after endlessly wallowing in
frustration and resentment over something that was clearly out of her
control, Alice has finally learned to let go.

Now she lets go of all those unhelpful stories about how Jim should
have been a better conversationalist and how her life would be so much
better if he were different. She lets go of comparing Jim to her friends'
husbands, realizing it only fuels her dissatisfaction. It isn't that her mind
has stopped judging, comparing, and criticizing—it's just that she has
learned to hold these stories lightly, to recognize when she is hooked by
them, and then to unhook herself. She still at times feels frustrated or
disappointed. But she has learned to open up and make room for those
feelings instead of allowing them to control her.

At the same time, she doesn't neglect her own needs. She acknowledges her desire for stimulating conversation and looks for it elsewhere.
She has plenty of friends that she loves to talk with, and she chooses to
spend more time with them. None of this has turned Jim into a great
conversationalist, but it has removed a whole lot of useless tension from
their relationship.

The reality is your partner will never be able to meet all your needs.
There's no harm in trying to get them met, but make sure you are

mindful of the consequences. If you hold on too tightly to your own agenda, there will come a point where your attempts to get what you want will do more harm than good. Your challenge is to recognize when you've reached that point—and then let go. Inevitably this will take some trial and error, and there'll be plenty of times you get it wrong. So keep experimenting. Find the best possible balance. Don't become a puppy dog or a doormat; there's no vitality in that. But don't turn into a shark or a battering ram either; that's a surefire way to destroy your relationship. Instead, find the middle ground.

values vs. needs

One thing that often helps when the gap opens wide is to come back to your core values as a partner. A quick recap: values are your heart's deepest desires for what you want to do and what you want to stand for during your time on this planet. While there is no such thing as a "right" or "wrong" value, there are certain values that generally make relationships thrive, such as compassion, caring, connection, contribution, collaboration, honesty, and respect—to name but a few. But remember, values are desired behaviors, desired qualities of ongoing action. They are about what you want to *do* and keep on *doing*.

Let's suppose that "respect" is really important to you. Then ask yourself, "What do I want to *do* about it?" Here are some possibilities:

- Treat others with respect.

- Ask others to treat you with respect.

- Thank others when they treat you with respect.

- Build relationships with other people who think respect is important.

- Refuse to talk to or interact with others when they treat you disrespectfully.

- Talk about the importance of respect.

You may have noticed something here. You can act on any of these values at any time. You can act on these values regardless of whether or not you actually get respect.

Values and needs are very different. Values are about what you want to *do*, whereas needs are about what you want to *get*. Here are some needs around respect:

- I need my partner to treat me with respect.

- I need my partner to respect my wishes.

- I need my partner to respect my opinions.

Notice that these things are all out of your control. There is simply no way to make your partner do these things. You can ask him nicely. You can ask him aggressively. You can ask him scornfully. You can yell at her. You can beg her. You can abuse her. You can threaten to divorce him. You can actually divorce her. But you cannot make your partner do what you want.

This is the reality we all face. We can take control of what we do, but we have no control over what we get. And while we can increase the likelihood of getting our needs met, we can only do this by taking control of what we do, such as asking nicely.

Because we can only take control of what we do, here's the four-step plan that I often recommend to my clients:

1. Try a wide variety of workable strategies to get your needs met (and stop using the unworkable ones).

2. If you've tried every workable strategy you can think of and your needs remain unmet, then you'll need to make a choice about staying or leaving. (You might like to revisit chapter 3.)

3. If you do choose to stay, then your best option is to practice acceptance, make the most of it, and enrich your life through living by your values.

4. The worst option is to stay but refuse to accept reality. Instead of making the most of it and living by your values, you waste your time and energy on worrying, brooding,

rehashing the past, fighting, complaining, criticizing, dwelling on what's wrong, taking drugs or alcohol, overeating, worrying, and so on.

Strategies in Action: Antonio and Maria

Antonio and Maria are a middle-aged couple, married with three adult children. Maria wants to have sexual intercourse at least once a week, but Tony prefers sex once a month. Maria has tried criticizing him, pleading with him, insulting him, dressing up sexily, demanding sex from him, reminding him of his "duties as a man," telling him about the sex lives of her friends, comparing him to her friends' husbands, telling him she feels unloved, asking him to make her "feel like a real woman," and so on. She's been doing this for years with no benefit. In fact, the more pressure Maria applies, the more Antonio loses interest in sex and the less frequently it happens.

When we look at Maria's values underlying sex, they include these:

■ Generating sexual pleasure

■ Creating sensual physical experiences

■ Connecting at a deep level

Notice these are values, not needs; they are all about doing, not getting.

The next step is a collaborative brainstorming session. We brainstorm as many ways as possible that Maria can act on these values, instead of focusing on the unmet need of sexual intercourse. Here's what we come up with:

■ Generating sexual pleasure: Maria recognizes that she can do this by herself, without Antonio, through masturbation. In fact, many women report that they have better orgasms through masturbation than they do through intercourse (Hite 1976).

■ Creating sensual physical experiences: Maria realizes she can also do this by herself by having a massage, spa bath, or facial.

■ Connecting at a deep level: Maria comes up with all sorts of ways of connecting deeply that do not involve having sexual intercourse. She can connect deeply with herself through journaling, meditation, yoga, or mindful breathing. She can connect at a deep level with friends and relatives by building close, intimate relationships. And she can connect deeply with Antonio in many ways that do not involve having sex: from holding hands and cuddling to having meaningful heart-to-heart conversations.

Once we finish our brainstorming session, I summarize all the different ways that Maria can act on her values around sex despite the fact she isn't having intercourse. Her initial reaction is not too positive. Here's how the conversation goes:

Maria: (*protesting*) Yes, I can see there are lots of other things I can do, but that's not the same as having sex!

Russ: Of course it's not. It's not the same thing at all. Let's acknowledge there's a big gap here: a gap between what you've got and what you want. So what are the normal feelings that you would expect *anybody* to feel in your situation?

Maria: Well, some frustration, I suppose.

Russ: Absolutely. Frustration. Disappointment. Sadness. Anger. Possibly even feelings of rejection or loneliness. These are all normal feelings. This is what we feel when there's a gap between what we want and what we've got. So the question is, what do we do when those feelings show up? We can wallow in them, struggle with them, let them jerk us around like a puppet on a string. Or we can make room for them, let them be, and focus on living by our values, here and now. Which is more workable? Which would give you the greatest quality of life?

I am pleased that Maria quickly gets the point: that doing what works often gives rise to discomfort. Like Maria, when you let go of your agenda around a particular need, you are not likely to feel good about it—at least not in the short run. You will probably need to make room for some unpleasant thoughts and feelings. And your mind will tell you plenty of unhelpful stories, such as: *It's not fair. Why is he like this? If only ... Why should I have to ...?* You can't stop these thoughts from popping up. The choice you have is whether or not you latch on to them. Hold on tight, and they instantly turn into smog. Let them go, and the smog rapidly clears.

Now as it happens, once Maria is willing to let go of the need for intercourse, things improve dramatically. Once the pressure is taken off Antonio, he becomes far more willing to cooperate. He is very open to intimate, sensual experiences as long as Maria doesn't pressure him to have intercourse. So they start to do a lot more massaging, cuddling, and kissing. Maria is pleasantly surprised to find that they can connect just as deeply through cuddling, kissing, and talking as they can through having sex. They also make a deal that if Maria becomes highly aroused, she will masturbate rather than pressuring Antonio for sex. (And they both have to defuse from some very unhelpful stories around that!)

No Magic Wand

You can see, there is no magic wand here. However, if you're willing to take a step back from your needs and look instead at your values, you'll often be able to find some workable solutions. This is not always easy. On the contrary, it's often very difficult. The larger the gap between what you want and what you've got, the harder acceptance becomes. This is especially true when your partner betrays you or hurts you— which is why, in chapters to come, we're going to look at betrayal, trust, resentment, and forgiveness. But first we're going to look at another important factor for getting your needs met: something that has a huge impact not only on your relationship, but also on your own sense of well-being and fulfillment, something that requires you to ...

CHAPTER 18

open your eyes

Child: (pushing plate of food away) I don't want this.

Mother: (angrily) There are poor starving kids in Africa who don't get that much food to eat in a whole year!

Child: Well, give it to them then!

Did you ever have an encounter like this with your mother? I certainly did. Children are often unappreciative. And adults aren't much better. How often do we truly appreciate what we have? There is so much that we take for granted. A few years back, a friend of mine developed cancer in his neck. He was cured, but the radiation therapy destroyed the salivary glands in his mouth, so now he has to chew gum all day long to produce enough saliva to keep his mouth moist. When did you last stop to appreciate your own saliva? It lubricates your mouth, moistens your food, helps you digest what you eat. Yet most of the time, you hardly notice its presence. And yet, you sure notice its absence when your mouth goes dry!

And when did you last truly appreciate your immune system? All day long, it is firing on all cylinders, wiping out bugs of all shapes and sizes to ensure you remain fit and healthy. And we take it for granted, don't we? Until we come down with a virus. That's when we get the rude awakening. That's when we realize how good we usually have it.

And how good do we feel when we finally recover? For maybe an entire day, or even two days, we truly appreciate our health and well-being. But all too quickly, we take it for granted again.

We do this with virtually every aspect of our life. We take our hands for granted—until they get injured. We take our eyes for granted—until we need glasses. We take our memory for granted—until it falters. We fail to appreciate just how much these things contribute to our quality of life. Where would we be without hands, eyes, or memory? We meet someone who is blind or missing a limb, or we visit a relative with dementia, and in those moments we may appreciate what we have, but it doesn't last long.

A few weeks ago, I was walking along a riverbank, and I was caught up in a story about getting old: "I used to be able to walk so much faster than this. And now my knees creak and my back aches. And I'm only forty-two years old!" I didn't notice the old guy on his walking stick until he called out to me. He laughed and shouted, "I wish I could walk as fast as you!" That literally stopped me in my tracks. I chuckled and went on my way with a different attitude, marveling at how well my legs were still carrying me after forty-two years of pounding the planet.

So what has this got to do with relationships? Well, just about everything! How do you feel when you are ignored, dismissed, or taken for granted? We are all very similar under the skin. We all want to be acknowledged and appreciated for what we give. When others show appreciation, we feel valued; we feel as if our efforts are noticed and that we make a difference. And if they don't show appreciation, we feel, well, a whole range of things from irritation and disappointment to loneliness or sadness; it seems as if what we do just doesn't mean very much to other people.

The word "appreciate" comes from the Latin words *ad* meaning "to" and *pretium* meaning "prize" or "value," so "appreciate" means "to value or prize something." No wonder we like to receive appreciation; how wonderful to be valued or prized by our partner! And our partner, of course, feels exactly the same way. So what would happen, do you think, if you showed your partner some more appreciation? Would your relationship improve or get worse? (As you reflect on this, see if you can catch your mind in the process of storytelling. Did it say something like any of the following? *He'll just take me for granted. All I ever do is give. It'll never be enough for her. I shouldn't have to …?* Would those be helpful stories to hold tightly?)

Appreciation is at the very heart of mindfulness. When we are on automatic pilot, we do not notice what we have. Unless some amazing new experience catches our eye, we pay little or no attention to the world around us. But if we bring awareness to this moment with an attitude of openness and curiosity, we can readily notice just how much we have. When we take time to appreciate what we have, we feel a sense of richness and fulfillment. If we don't do this, if we get caught up in our stories about what's missing or what's not good enough, then we feel a sense of lack or dissatisfaction. Caught up in our psychological smog, we lose sight of the amazing valley beyond.

Popular sayings such as "Stop and smell the roses" and "Count your blessings" point to this truth, but we've heard them so often that they now sound trite or corny. And even the most eloquent of words can never do justice to the actual experience. So enough talking: let's do a few simple mindfulness exercises instead, and in doing so, let's make the most of this opportunity to truly acknowledge and appreciate what we have.

---

mindful appreciation

The exercises that follow are designed to help you cultivate appreciation for all sorts of things that we commonly take for granted. Please do them slowly, savoring the experience. If you rush through them to get to the next chapter, then you have missed the whole point.

exercise: *mindfulness of hearing*

Read through all the instructions first, then put the book down and do the exercise.

For one minute, notice everything you can hear. "Stretch your hearing out" in all directions. Notice the most distant sounds. Also notice the sounds coming from your own body: your breathing, your clothes rustling. Whatever sounds you notice, listen as if you've never heard them before; notice the volume, pitch, rhythm, vibration, timbre.

After you have listened mindfully for one minute, take a moment to appreciate your hearing. How much does it contribute to your life?

exercise: *mindfulness of breathing*

Read through all the instructions first, then put the book down and do the exercise.

For one minute, focus on your breathing. Empty your lungs and allow them to fill by themselves. Notice the breath flowing in and flowing out. Observe the act of breathing as if you've never encountered anything like it before; notice what happens in your nostrils, throat, shoulders, chest, and tummy.

After mindfully breathing for one minute, take a moment to appreciate that you can breathe. How much does breathing contribute to your life?

exercise: *mindfulness of seeing*

Read through all the instructions first, then put the book down and do the exercise.

For one minute, look around you and notice what you can see. Pick some familiar sights and look more closely. Notice areas of shadow and light; notice where there are clear borders and edges, and where there are not. Pick a familiar object and look at it as if you've never seen an object like that before. Notice the shape, color, and surface: is it shiny or dull, smooth or rough?

After looking mindfully for one minute, take a moment to appreciate that you can see. How much does sight contribute to your life?

exercise: *mindfulness of tasting*

Read through all the instructions first, then put the book down and do the exercise.

Pick a small morsel of food: a peanut or raisin, a small square of chocolate, or half a rice cracker. Close your eyes and place this food in your mouth. Let it rest on your tongue for a few moments, without chewing. Notice how your mouth salivates. Chew the food as slowly as you can, noticing every element of taste and texture. Study the flavor as if you have never tasted anything like it. Savor it as if you were starving.

Now take a moment to appreciate your tongue and your mouth. How much does the ability to eat, chew, and taste contribute to your life?

exercise: *the stage show*

Imagine that right now you are in the front row of a magnificent stage show. On the stage, there is everything that you can see, hear, smell, taste, touch, feel, and think. So far we've looked at only a few elements of the show; there's a lot more going on. Now, following the same structure as the previous exercises, take a few minutes to notice some of the other parts of the show:

- What you are doing with your hands

- What you can sense against your skin

- What you are thinking

- What you are feeling in your body

In each case, take a moment to appreciate what this adds to your life. Please do this now, before reading on.

So there you have it. You're always in the midst of an amazing stage show, which is composed of sight, sound, smell, taste, touch, thoughts, and feelings. And isn't it astounding that you are able to witness this show? Isn't it amazing that your eyes and ears and arms and legs and mouth and brain all work together to keep this show continually running and changing? In his book *The Miracle of Mindfulness*, Buddhist monk and Nobel Peace Prize nominee Thich Nhat Hanh writes, "The real miracle is not to walk on water or in thin air, but to walk on earth. Every day we are engaged in a miracle which we don't even recognize: a blue sky, white clouds, green leaves, the black, curious eyes of a child—our own two eyes. All is a miracle."

the art of appreciation

At times, appreciation comes naturally. When you're hungry and someone feeds you, when you're cold and you turn on the heater, when someone does you a favor, when you taste a really good wine or piece of chocolate—in these moments, appreciation happens spontaneously. But most of the time, our mind lulls us into a state of disconnection. We fail to appreciate the magnificent ever-changing stage show of life. Our mind creates a T-shirt with the slogan: "Been there! Done that! Seen the movie! Read the book!" Then it pulls that T-shirt over our head and leaves it there.

Mindfulness is like peeling this T-shirt off so you can see the world with new eyes. If you use mindfulness to cultivate appreciation for your partner, then both of you will benefit. The more you notice the many ways your partner contributes to your life, the more satisfied you will feel in your relationship. And the more your partner feels appreciated, the more he is likely to turn to you with warmth and kindness.

Many people, during periods of conflict and tension, fantasize about breaking up with their partner. And if it actually happens, for a small minority, it comes as a welcome relief. But for many, it is a huge shock: breaking up is far more stressful than they ever imagined. On the brink of divorce, facing life alone, a man often starts to appreciate his wife and to recognize just how much she brings into his life. Or a woman starts to appreciate her husband and to realize how much he contributes to her well-being and lifestyle. Why do we so often wait until the point of no return before we learn to see what our partner gives us? Answer: psychological smog. When you're trapped inside-your-mind, entangled in a million different stories, you fail to appreciate what you have right in front of your eyes.

Joe, an accountant, took his wife, Claire, for granted. He even judged her harshly for choosing to be a homemaker instead of a career woman. But all that changed when she got cancer. As Claire became sicker and Joe had to take over looking after the kids, maintaining the house, doing the laundry, and putting dinner on the table, he started to appreciate just how much Claire did for him and his family. He also began to recognize the million and one ways she enriched his life: the kisses, the conversation, the intimacy, the friendship, the support, the companionship. Fortunately Claire survived, and their relationship grew much stronger through the experience. Many others are not so lucky. I've had numerous clients tell me that they only truly appreciated their partner once it was too late. There's an old English proverb that points to this: "We never know the worth of water 'til the well runs dry."

The message is loud and clear: if you don't bother to look, you will not see. Mindfulness means opening your eyes wide, seeing your partner clearly, and acknowledging what she adds to your life. If you're lucky, your mind will remind you to do this. However, your mind is far more likely to tell you how she detracts from your life. After all, your mind has been doing this for years, so it's not going to change its ways now just because you've read a book! It will tell you story after story about all the things your partner does "wrong." And if you hold onto them tightly, the smog soon thickens until you lose sight of your partner. So you know the drill: acknowledge those thoughts when they appear, and then let them come and go like passing cars.

Appreciating Your Partner

Following are a few suggestions to cultivate appreciation of your partner:

■ Each day notice (at least) three things you appreciate about your partner. They don't have to be big things; they can be tiny. It might be the way he smiles, or the way he describes things, or the warmth of his body beside you in the morning. It might be the way she walks, or the kiss she gives you on the cheek, or the sound of her laughter.

■ Contemplate what your partner adds to your life. If you're stuck for ideas, consider these questions: If my partner were on his deathbed, what would I tell him I appreciated most about him? If my partner died, what would I find hardest about living alone?

■ Each day notice (at least) three ways in which your partner contributes to your life. Again, they don't have to be big things; they can be tiny. It might be the simple fact that she goes to work to earn money to help pay for some of the things you enjoy having. Or the simple pleasure of having someone to talk to over dinner. Or the feeling of added security you have when you're not alone.

■ Think back to when you first met your partner: what personal qualities and strengths did she have? What did he say or do that made him attractive? In all likelihood, those strengths and qualities are still there today; you're just not noticing them anymore. Each day notice (at least) three things your partner says or does that are representative of her personal strengths and qualities.

■ At the end of each day, write down in your journal or worksheet whatever you have noticed in these exercises.

Don't Just Appreciate: Say Something!

Appreciating your partner will add to your own sense of fulfillment and satisfaction, but what about her? How will she know you appreciate her? Sure, she may notice some positive changes in you: perhaps you'll seem warmer, more open, more accepting, more affectionate, or less grumpy, irritable, judgmental, or critical. But she may not have the slightest idea why. So how about telling her? You know how good it feels when someone acknowledges your contribution, so why not give that pleasure to your partner? Here are a few examples:

"I really appreciate the way you look after the house."

"Thank you for working so hard to help us have this lifestyle."

"I'm so glad you're in my life. Thank you for being here."

"I love feeling your body next to me in bed."

"I appreciate the efforts you're making with my parents. I know how hard it is for you."

"Thank you for taking the time to read this book and do these exercises. I know this isn't really your thing. It means a lot to me that you're willing to make the effort."

"I really enjoyed it last night when you cuddled with me in bed."

This may not come naturally to you at first, but it's worth persisting until it does. And keep in mind, you can show appreciation without words. You might stroke your partner, or hug him, or give him a kiss. You might cook her a meal, buy her some flowers, or make her a cup of tea. Words, however, are important. For most people, they carry a lot of weight. So don't avoid using them just because you feel awkward or uncomfortable.

Another thing: if your partner does start saying these sorts of things to you, make sure you respond positively. Your mind may tell you stories—*He doesn't really mean that* or *He's just saying it because he read it in the book*. But let those stories go. Don't make the same mistake as Eleanor. When Rob started telling her how much he appreciated her, she completely undermined him. She would say things like "You sound so insincere. Say it like you mean it." But Rob was sincere. His voice may have sounded odd because he was embarrassed. He was learning a new way to talk, and he felt uncomfortable—but he did mean every word that he said. Sure enough, after a few of these put-downs from Eleanor, Rob stopped trying. The moral of the story? If your partner makes the effort to appreciate you, then make sure you appreciate his efforts.

Expressing appreciation for your partner can pay huge dividends. Not only does it bring you closer together, it also allows you to positively influence her behavior. How so? Through a principle commonly known as "carrot versus stick."

Carrot vs. Stick

Do you like carrots? Personally I'm not too keen on them. But then I'm not a donkey. Donkeys absolutely love carrots. So if you have a pet donkey and you want it to carry a heavy load for you, then one simple way to motivate it is by dangling a carrot in front of its nose. An alternative way is to beat it with a stick. Both methods will get the donkey moving—but over time, if you always rely on the stick, your donkey will turn into a sad, battered beast. In contrast, if you motivate your donkey with carrots, over time, you'll have a happy, healthy companion.

When it comes to motivation, humans are not that different from donkeys. Did you ever have a coach, teacher, mentor, or parent who noticed the things you did right, who commented on your improvements, and who praised you for making progress? Did you ever have one who only noticed what you did wrong or what wasn't good enough? How did the two compare?

Unfortunately, in trying to motivate our partner, we tend to use the stick far more than the carrot. The stick comes in a variety of different forms: from judging, criticizing, and blaming to shouting, threatening, and withdrawing. None of these approaches are workable; they may sometimes get your partner moving in the short run, but they won't improve your relationship in the long run.

Catch Them Doing It Right

No matter how much strife there is in your relationship, there are surely some things your partner does that you approve of. So see if you can catch him in the act. Whenever he does something you approve of, notice it, acknowledge it, and let him know you appreciate it. By doing this regularly, there's a good chance that this behavior will increase. Why? Simply because humans like to be noticed, acknowledged, and appreciated by the people they care about, so they tend to do more of whatever makes this more likely.

Many people react negatively to this idea. It seems to go against the grain. This is largely because of our upbringing. Most of us as children only got rewarded when we did things the way our parents wanted. And if we didn't do it like Mom or Dad wanted, we probably got punished. Our schools worked on much the same system. So the idea of rewarding your partner when he doesn't do things exactly as you want might seem somewhat odd, but it is based on a wealth of scientific evidence.

For decades, behavioral psychologists have studied how to influence the behavior of animals. Their findings are consistent across a wide range of different species, from rats to monkeys to humans. The most effective way to change an animal's behavior is to give five times as many rewards as punishments. In other words, if you want to positively influence your partner's behavior, you will need to praise her five times as much as you criticize her. Yes, you read that correctly—*five* times more praise than criticism. Does this seem outrageous? It certainly did to Jed.

One of Yvonne and Jed's "pet arguments" was housework. Jed liked to keep the house spectacularly tidy. Yvonne liked a reasonably tidy house, but she didn't share the same high standards as Jed. She had a tendency to leave books on the dining room table, shoes on the living room floor, coats on the backs of chairs, and unwashed dishes in the sink. This really got Jed's goat. "Why can't you just pick up after yourself?" he'd ask in an irritable voice. "It's not that hard. Why do you have to leave all this stuff lying around the place?"

"I don't notice it," Yvonne would protest.

"It's not that hard," Jed would snap. "Just open your eyes." Often when he got home from work, he'd wander around the house, tidying up Yvonne's mess, grumbling about how lazy she was. He was so caught up in the "lazy wife" story, he failed to appreciate the many ways that Yvonne *did* help out. If Yvonne put her shoes away eight times out of ten, Jed only noticed the two times that she didn't. If Yvonne washed up two nights a week, Jed only noticed the five nights that she didn't. If Yvonne occasionally pulled out the vacuum and cleaned the carpets, Jed merely thought, "It's about time she lifted a finger to help!" Jed's strategy is extremely ineffective, for two main reasons:

1. By constantly focusing on what Yvonne does *not* do, he increases his own frustration and dissatisfaction.

2. The most effective way to get Yvonne to do more housework is to notice all those times that she *does* do it and to tell her how much he appreciates it. That will likely make her feel valued, and therefore she may be motivated to do more of it in the future.

How did Jed feel when we discussed this? Not too happy:

Jed: But I shouldn't have to do all that! She should just do it naturally. I thought women were supposed to be tidier than men.

Russ: That's a common reaction. Did you notice the "should" there? Let me ask you, when you hold on tight to "Yvonne should be tidier," what happens to your relationship?

Jed: It gets worse.

Russ:	So here's the thing; your mind will tell you again and again and again, "Yvonne should be tidier," or something along those lines, right? I mean, how long has your mind been telling you some version of that story?
Jed:	Ever since we met, I guess.
Russ:	Right. So it's not likely to stop telling you anytime soon, is it?
Jed:	No, because it's true. She *should* be tidier.
Russ:	Well, millions of people would agree with you. But that would have no effect whatsoever on improving the situation. The question is, when this thought shows up, is it helpful to get caught up in it? Is it helpful to dwell on it? Is it helpful to let this thought dictate how you treat her?
Jed:	No.
Russ:	Okay. So can you name that story when it shows up and then let it go?
Jed:	I guess so.
Russ:	Well, this isn't a quiz show. There's nothing to guess. It's just a simple question: is that a story you're willing to let go of, regardless of whether it's true?
Jed:	I want to say yes, but I don't feel like I can.
Russ:	So check your experience: for ten years, you've been getting caught up in that story—has it brought you happiness or brought you closer together?
Jed:	No.
Russ:	Has it changed Yvonne's behavior in any lasting way?
Jed:	No.
Russ:	So then, is it helpful for you to hold on to it?
Jed:	I guess not. But it's hard to just let go of it, just like that.
Russ:	Sure. Absolutely. This stuff is hard. The question is, is it worth making the effort?
Jed:	Well, when you put it like that—yes.

Letting go turned out to be a huge challenge for Jed. Over the next few weeks, there were countless occasions where he wanted to criticize Yvonne and point out all the things she was not doing. But instead he dropped anchor and kept his mouth shut. He practiced naming his judgmental thoughts and was shocked to see how many he had in one day. He practiced breathing into and making room for his frustration. And he started to employ positive reinforcement. If Yvonne placed her coat on the coat rack instead of the chair, he'd say, "Thanks, Yvonne. I appreciated that." If she put the dishes in the dishwasher, he'd say, "Thanks for loading the dishwasher." If she made the bed, he'd say, "Thank you for making the bed. It makes life so much easier."

Over time Yvonne's tidying behaviors started to increase. Why? Well, first, she appreciated Jed's efforts to notice and acknowledge her contributions. That built some goodwill and motivated her to try harder. Second, the amount of fighting and tension decreased, which made her feel more warm and open—and therefore naturally more attentive to Jed's wishes. It's unlikely that Yvonne and Jed will ever have the same standards of tidiness and cleanliness. But they do have a better balance now. Yvonne is tidier than she was. Jed is more accepting than he was. It works better for both of them. It'll never be perfect—but then again, what is?

CHAPTER 19

sticky situations

Question: "What happens when an irresistible force meets an unmovable object?"

Gets your mind whirring, doesn't it? I don't know the answer, but one thing's for sure: when this starts to happen in a relationship, both partners suffer. Here are some common scenarios where this happens:

- One partner wants children, but the other doesn't.

- One partner wants to live overseas, but the other doesn't.

- One partner wants to get married, but the other doesn't.

- One partner wants a religious upbringing for their children, but the other doesn't.

- One partner wants frequent sexual intercourse, but the other doesn't.

These are sticky, complicated, painful, messy situations, and they rarely, if ever, have simple answers. The great playwright George Bernard Shaw put it like this: "For every complex problem, there is a simple solution that is wrong." Now your mind does not like this idea. It will generally go into overdrive trying to find a solution: analyze,

analyze, analyze; ponder, ponder, ponder. But your mind is not likely to be successful. Don't take my word for it: check your experience. If you are currently in a sticky situation, consider this: How much time have you spent trying to resolve it? How much time have you wasted inside-your-mind—worrying, stewing, pondering, analyzing, or brooding? And what effect is that having on your relationship? The sad thing is, when we get caught up in these dilemmas, our partner starts to seem like she is our enemy, which only makes the situation worse.

The harsh reality is this: *Sticky situations do not have easy answers!* Can you accept this reality? Life has dumped this on your doorstep. You didn't expect it; you didn't ask for it; you didn't want it. But here it is. This is what life delivered. It's difficult, it's painful, it's unfair. But you can't send it back. So can you open up to this reality and make space for the painful feelings that go with it? And can you make some positive use of your pain? "What?!" you ask. "Are you crazy?!" Well, no—though it may seem like it. One of the things that pain is very useful for is helping you develop something called …

compassion

The word "compassion" comes from two ancient Latin terms: *com*, which means "together," and *pati*, which means "to bear or suffer." Thus "compassion" literally means "suffering together." In its modern usage, the word has a much more complex meaning. Compassion involves noticing and paying attention to the suffering of another living being with a spirit of kindness and caring and a genuine desire to help, nurture, or support.

For most of us, compassion comes naturally under extreme circumstances. For example, we may feel compassion when we watch the news and we see young children starving in Ethiopia; or a mother crying over the lifeless body of her young son amid a pile of rubble in war-torn Iraq; or the survivors of the September 11 attacks sharing their horrific first-hand accounts of loved ones jumping to their deaths. Closer to home, we are often spontaneously compassionate when our friends or relatives face a major life crisis: death, illness, injury, trauma, or divorce.

However, on a day-to-day basis, we easily lose touch with compassion—for ourselves and for others. And this is problematic. Without compassion for others, we all too readily turn a blind eye to their pain and suffering. Without compassion, it becomes easy to judge others, to look down on them, scorn them, neglect them, reject them, or hurt them. Without compassion, we look on our fellow human being as little more than an object instead of as a real person. And what effect does that have on our relationships? What happens when you treat a human as an object? What happens when you treat *yourself* as an object?

developing self-compassion

Compassion for yourself is equally important as compassion for others. The more you can develop self-compassion, the easier it is to be compassionate toward others—so everybody wins. Dr. Kristin Neff, a psychology professor at the University of Texas, has researched this topic extensively (Neff 2003). Neff suggests there are three elements for developing self-compassion: kindness, common humanity, and mindfulness. Let's take a look at each of these in more detail.

Kindness

As we go through life, we will screw up and make mistakes. We will get caught up in unhelpful beliefs. No matter how much we develop our mindfulness skills, there will be times when we forget to use them. We will act in self-defeating ways, and we will hurt the very people we love the most. At times, we will feel inadequate, stupid, foolish, unlovable, or not good enough. Naturally, this hurts.

Wouldn't it be great if, during those times of suffering, you could reach out to someone who unconditionally accepts you? Someone who sees you as you are, with all your human foibles and flaws and weaknesses, but does not judge or condemn or criticize you? Someone who basically says, "Hey, I'm here for you. Let me help. I can see you're in pain. You're hurting. Whatever you need, I'm here for you"? Self-compassion means reaching out to yourself with acceptance, warmth, and understanding. It is an act of great kindness.

Common Humanity

Often when you're suffering, your mind tells you that you are the only one suffering, that everybody else out there is happier than you are, that others don't feel as much pain as you, that others don't screw up or fail as much as you do. But if you clutch this story tightly, it will only make your suffering worse. If you're feeling guilty, fearful, angry, inadequate, lonely, ashamed, or resentful, it can be helpful to remember these are all normal human experiences. All over the planet, in this moment, there are millions upon millions of other humans suffering in ways very similar to your own.

The reality is all humans suffer. Not all to the same degree, of course. Poverty-stricken children growing up in war-torn third-world countries are likely to suffer much more than Western kids growing up in wealthy middle-class suburbia. But that's not the point. The point is to recognize you are human. Every human life will be touched by loss, rejection, failure, frustration, and disappointment. Every human being will lose their temper and do things they regret. Every human being will screw up. The more you can recognize this and accept your own humanity, the more you will be able to treat yourself kindly and gently.

Mindfulness

You already know a lot about mindfulness, and hopefully are practicing it more and more. When we make room for our painful feelings and defuse from our punitive, self-critical stories, then this is yet another act of kindness.

Tips for Self-Compassion: Putting It All Together

Here are some tips for developing self-compassion:

Start with mindful breathing. Breathe slowly and deeply. Breathe into your body, wherever it hurts most. Imagine your breath flowing into and around the pain; feel yourself opening up around it.

Place a hand on the area that is most painful. Imagine this is a healing hand—the hand of a loving doctor, nurse, or parent. Feel the warmth flow from your hand to your body. Imagine your body softening around the pain. Hold the pain gently, as if it is an injured puppy or a crying baby.

Talk kindly to yourself. Suppose someone you love were suffering in the very same way as you are; what would you say to let them know that you care? Try saying these very same words to yourself.

Imagine yourself as a young child. Imagine that child is hurting as much as you. What might you say to him, if you wanted to let him know how much you care? Say something similar to yourself, with the same attitude of care, concern, and kindness.

Acknowledge that you're human. If you're beating yourself up for screwing up, then remind yourself, "Yes. I'm a human being. Like everybody else on the planet, I am imperfect."

Draw on your curiosity. Ask yourself, "What does this teach me about what it is to be human?" and "What insight does this give me into friends, family, and all other humans that suffer?"

Remember what your pain tells you. This pain tells you three important things:

1. You're alive: that's a good start.

2. You're human: this is what humans feel when they suffer.

3. You have a heart: if you didn't care about anything, you wouldn't be having these painful feelings.

Self-compassion won't solve these painful issues, but it will help you to cope much better with the stress. Then you can focus on … getting unstuck.

getting unstuck

Getting unstuck from sticky situations like those mentioned at the beginning of the chapter is obviously easier said than done. The suggestions that follow should not be seen as "solutions." They are simply ideas that may help you respond more effectively to such difficult issues so you can find some vitality within your pain.

Bring In Some LOVE

How can the LOVE formula—letting go, opening up, valuing, engaging—help you? Are you lost in psychological smog? What unhelpful stories can you loosen your grip on? Are you holding on to "I'm right, you're wrong," "bad partner," "too hard," or "it's hopeless"? Can you open up and make room for your painful feelings? Can you live by your values, even as you wade through this sticky mess? Can you engage fully in your life and your relationship, even though you're caught in a painful conflict?

Connect with Your Values

Chances are whatever your sticky issue is, you'll be discussing it for a while. So how do you want to behave as you have those discussions? Do you want to act with openness, honesty, compassion, caring, and respect? Or do you want to act with hostility, deceit, disconnection, avoidance, and contempt? If you can tune in to your core values, your heart-to-heart talks will go more smoothly. Instead of turning your partner into an enemy, she becomes a friend with whom you don't agree.

Extend Compassion

Extend compassion to both you and your partner. Openly acknowledge how hard this situation is. Reveal to each other how much you are hurting. Can you acknowledge your partner's pain, and think and act

181

kindly toward him, knowing that he is hurting just like you? When you fell in love, you never anticipated this issue. Now you're both trapped in the reality gap: squashed up, hardly able to breathe, squeezing the life from each other. Neither of you wanted this. Both of you need and deserve some care and kindness.

Try On the Moccasins

There's a famous American Indian proverb that says, "Never judge a man until you walk a mile in his moccasins." When painful dilemmas arise, the psychological smog rapidly thickens. One way out is to consciously look at things from your partner's perspective. This doesn't mean you have to agree with her; you just try to understand where she's coming from. If you can truly put yourself in her shoes (or moccasins), you are less likely to judge her harshly and more likely to loosen your grip on "I'm right, you're wrong." Also, when you take the time to see things from her point of view, she will feel valued or respected, which sets the scene for a more fruitful interaction. This is a basic principle, taught in all negotiation and communication classes. Stephen Covey, author of *The 7 Habits of Highly Effective People*, summarized it succinctly: "Seek first to understand, then to be understood."

The first step is to put yourself in your partner's shoes. What is he afraid of? What ideas and assumptions is she holding on to? How old are these thoughts? When did they start? What does he want for the future? What is she afraid will happen if she does what you desire? Why does that matter to her?

The second step is to see if you've got it right. You could say something like, "I've been trying to see this from your point of view, and I'd like you to tell me if I've understood you correctly. What you want is A, B, and C, but what you're afraid of is D, E, and F. Is that right?"

The third step is to continue this conversation until your partner feels you understand his viewpoint. Doing this sends a powerful message: "I'm interested in you. Help me understand. Let's work this out as partners, not enemies." It is an act of both caring and connection. It won't necessarily change the situation, but it creates a better atmosphere for ongoing talks.

Find the Gold in the Garbage

Sometimes it's good to be selfish. When life dumps a load of garbage on you, ask yourself, "What's in this for me?" That may seem like an odd question, but it has the potential to transform your entire life. If you're willing to look, you'll find gold in the midst of that garbage. Every problem in life brings an opportunity to learn and grow, to develop personal strengths such as mindfulness, acceptance, letting go, persistence, and patience. We don't want to have these painful issues, but when they are thrust upon us, we might as well get something useful out of them. For example, we can use our own suffering to develop compassion, which helps us connect with and be there for others who need us. Kelly Wilson, one of the founders of ACT, talks about how your own suffering enables you to develop an "emotional stethoscope" with which you can hear the pain in the hearts of others.

The comedienne Rita Rudner said, "I love being married. It's so great to find that one special person you want to annoy for the rest of your life." This humorous quip reveals a potent truth: in any relationship, there will be things you do that upset your partner—and vice versa. You are different people with different family backgrounds, different ways of thinking, and different ways of doing things. Sooner or later, those differences will create tension and conflict. But no matter how bad it gets, you can—with the right attitude—gain some benefit. Every sticky situation is an opportunity to develop psychological flexibility. Therefore, ask yourself repeatedly, "How can I grow or develop throughout this process?"

Sir Winston Churchill said it like this: "A pessimist sees the difficulty in every opportunity; an optimist sees the opportunity in every difficulty." So imagine that your partner is a highly paid, live-in personal trainer and that you have paid her a small fortune to help you develop some important life skills. Her methods are unconventional, and at times they drive you nuts. But you want to get your money's worth. So what important life skills can she help you develop? Mindfulness, acceptance, forgiveness, letting go, assertiveness, compassion, patience? This attitude won't make you like or want the garbage, but it will help you discover the gold inside it.

CHAPTER 20

the christmas truce

It is World War I, the winter of 1914. The Germans have been fighting the British and French for months. Already hundreds of thousands of soldiers have died on both sides, and the war is only a few months old. You're a British soldier on the battlefields of Flanders, Belgium. You're cold, wet, hungry, dirty, exhausted; you're living in a muddy trench infested with rats; you're a long way from home and frightened of dying. And as the night grows dark and bitterly cold, you can't believe tomorrow is Christmas Day. Suddenly you see a glow above the German trenches. You can't believe your eyes. It's a Christmas tree, decorated with candles. And the Germans are singing carols that you recognize— in a completely different language but the same tunes!

In his book *Silent Night: The Story of the World War I Christmas Truce*, Stanley Weintraub describes what happened next: "After a few trees were shot at, the British became more curious than belligerent and crawled forward to watch and listen. And after a while, they began to sing. By Christmas morning, the 'no man's land' between the trenches was filled with fraternizing soldiers, sharing rations and gifts, singing and (more solemnly) burying their dead between the lines. Soon they were even playing soccer" (Weintraub 2001).

"The Christmas Truce" has to be one of the most amazing episodes in human history. Rival armies that had been killing each other mercilessly for months put down their weapons, climbed out of their trenches, and made friends. They sang songs and exchanged gifts; shared cigarettes, chocolate cake, and cognac; they played soccer on frozen mud with empty food cans. Sadly the truce didn't last more than a few days. But that does not detract from the nature of this event. It shows clearly that even in the midst of a bloodthirsty battle, there is always the potential to connect with your core human values.

patching up

We can all learn from this story. At times, we get so embroiled in conflict with our partner that we lose touch with our heart. Armed to the teeth with anger, resentment, and bitterness, we charge into battle, intent on winning at any cost. Or we huddle in our trench, waiting for the opportunity to strike. There is no vitality in this stance. We merely end up miserable, lonely, and exhausted.

Fortunately there is hope. We can at any moment declare a truce. We can, if we wish, stop fighting and reach out to our partner; we can make an effort to repair the damage done. And the more we choose to do so, the better for both of us. Each attempt we make to stop the fight, reach out, patch up, and reconnect sends a powerful message: "I care about you!" It connects us with our heart and reminds us of what this relationship is all about.

While this makes sense intuitively, it's good to know it's backed up with solid research. Earlier in the book, I mentioned the extensive research done by John Gottman. His data shows very clearly that one of the key factors in making a relationship thrive is the ability to send and receive frequent "repair attempts" (Gottman and Silver 1999). By "repair attempts," he means any words, actions, or gestures intended to repair the relationship. Gottman's research shows that even when couples fight a lot, if they are good at repairing, their relationship can still be very healthy. This is especially true for couples that fight fairly.

However, Gottman's data shows that it's not just the sending that matters; it's also the receiving. If you are mindful of these reparative words and gestures—if you notice them and appreciate them—then that enables bonding and healing. But if your partner reaches out and you push him away—if you close off, or keep attacking, or deflect, dismiss, or ignore his attempts to make up—then bonding and healing are not possible. Instead the wounds will grow deeper and start to fester.

There are many ways to send a repair attempt. Here are a few to get you thinking:

Reveal you're in pain. One way to stop the battle is simply by taking off your armor to show you're wounded. You could say, "Ouch," "I'm really hurting now," "I'm getting a headache," "I'm getting really stressed," "I'm feeling scared," or "I'm starting to feel a bit battered and bruised."

Ask for a cease-fire. A simple strategy is to ask directly for a truce. You could say: "Can we please take a rest?" "This is getting us nowhere." "I can't handle this. I need a break." "How about we take time out?" "Can we agree to disagree?" Or even "Can we just stop this and have a hug? I really need one right now."

Ask for better conditions. Another option is to continue the fight but change the fighting conditions, for example: "Can you please lower your voice?" "I'm happy to discuss this, but please don't yell." "That felt like it was below the belt. Can we please fight fairly here?" "Please stick to the topic." "Can you please say that again without all the judgments?"

Acknowledge the pointlessness. You might comment on the fact that the fighting is getting you nowhere, for example: "This is pointless, isn't it? We're getting nowhere." "We're expending a lot of time and effort here, aren't we?" "How much longer are we going to fight over this?" "This is like playing tug-of-war."

Use humor. Many of the defusion techniques in this book can be used with a dose of humor, for example: "The pet arguments are off the leash again." "I think my inner shark just got out." "We're both stuck in the 'I'm right, you're wrong' story." "I'm having the thought that I want to strangle you." If you and your partner did the exercise in chapter 15 where you name your fighting tactics, you can call them out: "I think you're exhuming the corpse" or "Good silverback display."

Try on the moccasins. As mentioned in the previous chapter, you can often improve the situation by making a concerted effort to see it from the other's point of view. You might say, "I don't understand where you're coming from. Please help me here," or "Let me see if I can get this from your point of view."

Offer an apology. When we fuse with "I'm right, you're wrong," saying sorry is the very last thing we want to do. Because of this, it can be very powerful and healing. Here are some possibilities of what you could say: "I'm sorry. I didn't mean to hurt you." "I'm sorry. I really screwed up badly." "Can we just press rewind here, and start again?" "I didn't intend it to come out like that. Will you let me try saying it differently?" "I did it again, didn't I? Sorry." "I can see how badly that hurt you. Can you forgive me, please?" "How can I set this right?" "What can I do to make up here?"

LOVE always comes first

In order to effectively send or receive a repair attempt, you need to be mindful. You won't be able to do it if you're trapped inside your mind or powering along full-throttle in reactivity mode. So LOVE comes first. Drop an anchor. Push your feet into the ground. Slow your breathing. Get present. Notice what your mind is telling you. Breathe into your feelings. Connect with your values. This only takes a few seconds. It's like pressing the pause button during a movie; for a few moments, the battle stops in its tracks. That few seconds is all the time you need to make a difference. Pause, breathe, and get present. Then engage once more—this time with a values-guided response.

The same holds true if you're on the receiving end. If you're lost in your own smog, you won't be able to see what your partner is doing. She's right there, waving the white flag around, but you just keep on shooting. You'll need to let go of unhelpful mind chatter like *She doesn't mean this*, or *This is her way of having a go at me*, or *Don't think you can get out of this that easily.* And if you spot anything that looks even remotely like a repair attempt, no matter how vague or fuzzy it appears through the smog, then pause, breathe, and acknowledge it. You might acknowledge it with a smile, a nod of your head, or by saying something like "Thanks," "I appreciate that," "Fair call," "I'm sorry too," or even "You're right, this is pointless. We're not getting anywhere." This may not come naturally, but it's an essential part of building a strong relationship.

if your partner is willing

The list of repair attempts given earlier in this chapter is by no means exhaustive. Brainstorm some things you might say or do that can de-escalate a conflict, help you recover and make up, or both. Here are three things to include in your brainstorming:

- Think back over old conflicts to see if you can recognize anything you said or did that helped to scale down the damage or quickly repair it.

- Agree on some words, phrases, and gestures you can use in the future to make repair attempts.

- Make a pact to be mindful of each other's repair attempts: to acknowledge them and accept them, even when you feel angry, hurt, or resentful.

a word of caution

Any and all of these techniques can backfire if your partner takes your words or gestures the wrong way. So make it clear that you're trying to patch things up. If necessary, spell it out literally: "I'm trying hard to patch things up here." Also be honest with yourself; if you're not mindful of your own intentions, you can easily subvert some of these comments into attacks, digs, jibes, and put-downs. So as you try these strategies, stay in touch with your values around connecting and caring. It's hard to do this while you're in the midst of a battle, but like everything, it gets easier with practice.

And if you forget everything in this book and you get bogged down in a really nasty fight, no problem: the moment you realize what's happened, you have several options. You could drop anchor and make repairs. Or you could disconnect and avoid. Or you could get lost inside-your-mind, brooding and seething. The choice is yours. But one thing's for sure: consistently choosing the first option will pay you major benefits in terms of ...

CHAPTER 21

intimacy

What's it all about? Why do you want to bother working on your relationship? What does it really matter to you? These are big questions, and there are no "right" answers. However, for most people, one major factor is the desire to be truly known and genuinely accepted. When someone sees us as we truly are behind all our pretenses, behind the show we put on for the world around us, behind that mask we wear in everyday life, and if, having seen those flaws and weaknesses we try so hard to hide, they continue to accept us and care for us, then we feel genuinely and deeply loved. Allowing someone to "see the real you" is commonly called "intimacy." The word "intimacy" is derived from the Latin *intimatio*, which means "to make known." Intimacy refers to a deep and close connection between two human beings. We can talk about it in at least three ways:

Physical intimacy: letting your partner know your body

Emotional intimacy: letting your partner know your feelings

Psychological intimacy: letting your partner know what's on your mind, including your values, goals, opinions, beliefs, desires, expectations, and fantasies

The deepest, closest relationships normally involve intimacy in all three of these areas. (However, this is not always so. It's important to remember each couple is unique, and there is no set formula as to what is "normal." Always come back to "workability" rather than "normality"; look at what works to enrich and deepen your own unique relationship, as opposed to what the "experts" say is normal.)

genuine intimacy: an act of willingness

Intimacy is a two-way street. For a true intimate connection, each of you needs to "make yourself known" to your partner. This cannot be forced or coerced. Genuine intimacy is an act of willingness; you willingly allow your partner to know you emotionally, physically, or psychologically. If you do this grudgingly or resentfully, or out of a sense of coercion or guilt or fear, it would be a destructive experience rather than a relationship-enhancing one.

Taking a Risk

To open up emotionally and psychologically is to take a risk. If you tell your partner how you are feeling or what you are thinking, you make yourself vulnerable to criticism, judgment, or disapproval. Your partner could easily criticize you. They might slap any number of harsh judgments on you from "weak and needy" to "selfish and greedy." They might avoid you or reject you. They might ridicule you or poke fun at you. They might even use this information to try to manipulate you or to deliberately hurt you.

Hopefully these things will not happen, but there's no guarantee. Indeed, some of the listed scenarios may have already happened in your current relationship or in previous ones. So when you open up to your partner, you are taking a genuine risk. And when humans take risks, they feel anxious (or fearful, edgy, uneasy, nervous, tense—whatever you prefer to call it). There is no way to avoid such feelings because, as discussed earlier in the book, we are hardwired to have a fight-or-flight reaction whenever we face a challenging situation. So the question is, are you willing to make room for your discomfort in order to build a closer, deeper relationship?

If your answer is no, then your relationship will inevitably lack intimacy. If your answer is yes, then it's wise to consider how you can minimize any risks involved. There's no point in being foolhardy or impetuous.

Making It Safe

One way to minimize the risk involved in intimacy is to move slowly, take "baby steps," and observe how your partner responds. Think about tiny ways in which you might be a bit more intimate. Perhaps you might share a little of what you are feeling. For example, you might say "I'm a bit grumpy today," "I'm worried about XYZ," "I feel very in love with you," or "I'm furious about ABC." Or perhaps you might disclose a genuine opinion rather than holding your tongue or saying something you don't really believe. Or you might tell your partner some of your dreams or hopes or goals rather than keeping them to yourself.

As you take these small risks, notice your partner's reactions. If he responds with openness, caring, interest, and acceptance, those are good signs; they suggest you can trust him. If he responds with hostility, withdrawal, contempt, disinterest, or rejection, those are not good signs; such reactions will only destroy trust.

The same holds true when the shoe is on the other foot. If your partner starts to open up to you, make it safe for her. Respond mindfully: pay attention with openness and curiosity. Tune into your values around contribution, connection, and caring. By making a "safe space" for your partner to open up, you contribute to her health and well-being, building a deep connection and showing that you care.

How do you create such a space? First, defuse from the judgments, criticisms, and other unhelpful stories that automatically pop into your head; simply notice these thoughts, and let them come and go. Second, engage: bring your full awareness to what your partner is saying and doing; make him the center of your attention. Third, show that you care. One particularly powerful way to do this is through a process called "validation."

Validating Your Partner's Feelings

Sometimes, in some situations, you and your partner will see eye-to-eye; you will have similar opinions and similar feelings about the issue. When this happens, you both feel united, aligned, supported. Often, however, this will not be the case. The likelihood is that you and your partner will often have differing opinions and feelings about a wide variety of subjects, issues, and situations. Sometimes these differences will be minor and sometimes vast. When this happens, watch out for "I'm right, you're wrong." Once hooked in by this story, you will act as if you have the "right" thoughts and feelings and your partner has the "wrong" ones. And how would that work in terms of building closeness and intimacy?

To *validate* your partner's feelings means simply that you acknowledge them and accept them. In other words, you understand that this is how your partner feels right now, and even though you feel differently, you respect her right to have her own individual thoughts and feelings. You cultivate an attitude of acceptance: "Your thoughts and feelings are different from mine; I may not like that difference, but I am willing to make room for it."

Naturally you will judge your partner's thoughts and feelings—to do so is human nature—but you can let those judgments go without holding on. And instead you can open yourself to the reality that this is how your partner sees the world; this is how she feels, and this is how she thinks. It's hardly surprising she sees things differently than you: you're two different people. And if you knew her in intimate detail, including her genetic and biological makeup, the structure of her brain and nervous system, and all the formative learning experiences she's ever had in her life, then the thoughts and feelings she has would seem perfectly natural and normal to you—even though they may be wildly different from your own.

Validation means you convey to your partner that it's all right for him to have his own unique thoughts and feelings, even though they're not the same as yours. If you're not willing to do this—if you cling to the story that your partner shouldn't feel or think like that—then what does this cost you? What impact does it have on your relationship? Validation is an important act of caring. It doesn't mean you agree with your partner; it doesn't mean you like or approve of the way he thinks and feels; it just means that you accept him and allow him to be who he is.

If you start attacking, criticizing, judging, challenging, minimizing, dismissing, or ignoring your partner's thoughts and feelings, this is "invalidating." Invalidating your partner's feelings is hurtful and destructive; it destroys trust and prevents intimacy. To truly validate your partner, you will not only need to let go of righteous ideas or judgments but also to make room for your own discomfort. Quite often, as your partner reveals her inner world, you will experience uncomfortable feelings. These may vary from anxiety and impatience to frustration or guilt. Your challenge is to open up enough so that your own discomfort can be there without a struggle.

Thus validation starts from a "headspace" of mindfulness. Then you follow up with words or actions. Actions can include anything from holding hands, to cuddling with your partner, to sitting quietly while paying mindful attention. Words can include:

"Ouch. That must hurt."

"It's natural you'd feel that way."

"This must be really hard for you."

"Tell me more."

"I'm here for you."

"This is tough for you. How can I help?"

These are just a few ideas. Why not discuss with your partner what sorts of actions and words each of you would find validating? Validation pays big dividends over time. Not least of which is ...

building a better sex life

Many people arbitrarily divide their relationship up into two parts: (1) their sex life and (2) everything else. This division is often unhelpful. It's generally more useful to think of sex as merely one activity that allows you to connect in a pleasurable way. Some people expect that despite a terrible ongoing relationship—full of disconnection, reactivity, and avoidance—they should be able to have a great sex life. Think again! While you could probably find rare exceptions, typically if there's significant DRAIN—disconnection, reactivity, avoidance, inside-your-mind, neglecting values—in your relationship, it negatively impacts your sex life. After all, if you can't connect lovingly outside the bedroom, why should it be any different inside?

As a general rule, if your sex life isn't good, first focus on reversing the DRAIN in other areas of your relationship. As you reestablish caring, connection, compassion, and trust, this paves the way for a better, more enjoyable sex life. Conversely, if you try to fix up your sex life while your relationship is fraught with tension, your chances of success are not very good. Once your relationship is thriving, you can then apply LOVE—letting go, opening up, valuing, and engaging—to enhance your sex life.

Sex and Letting Go

To enhance your sex life, what unhelpful expectations, rules, and judgments could you let go of? Here are some common ones:

- Your partner should like (or at least consent to) the same sexual activities as you.

- You or your partner should want to have sex more often/ less often.

- You or your partner should have a stronger erection or orgasm.

- You or your partner should get an erection or reach an orgasm more easily/more often/more quickly/more slowly.

If you fuse with these expectations, you'll repeatedly experience anxiety, frustration, or disappointment. Why? Because orgasms, erections, personal tastes, and sex drive all vary enormously—not only from person to person but from week to week and day to day. So if you grasp your expectations too tightly, it won't be long before you're struggling with reality.

When it comes to sex, "I'm right, you're wrong" often appears in the disguise of "I'm normal, you're abnormal." You're in for trouble if you get entangled in these stories, especially when it comes to foreplay, positions, masturbation, sex toys, or the "when, where, and how" of what you do. Clutch your stories tightly and you'll set yourself up for conflict rather than pleasure. And the same goes for judgments about performance, technique, or physical appearance.

It's natural to have these rules, expectations, and judgments, but if you won't loosen your grip on them, the smog will be so thick that you can't see your bedroom! So notice them, name them, and hold them lightly.

Sex and Opening Up

Are you willing to explore new ways (or revisit old ways) of enhancing your sex life? If so, I recommend *The New Joy of Sex* by Dr. Alex Comfort (see Recommended Reading). It's a book full of ideas to expand or improve your sex life. However, when you're trying out new things, rediscovering old things, or reengaging in sex after a long absence, there's a good chance you'll feel anxious, vulnerable, tense, embarrassed, or uncomfortable—at least initially. So are you open to those feelings? Can you make room for them in the service of better sex?

Of course, you also need to honor your values around self-care and self-respect. Don't do anything that would violate these funda-mental values. *Remember*: intimacy is an act of willingness. So if you are being coerced or forced into something against your will, that's not intimacy!

Sex and Valuing

What are your values underlying sex? Is it about connection, caring, sensuality, sharing physical pleasure, expressing your sexuality, affirming your love? Many people ruin their sex lives by turning sex into a goal-focused activity: it's all about the orgasm. While having an orgasm is generally a pleasurable experience, if it becomes "the be all and end all" of your sex life, sooner or later such an attitude will create problems. Why? Because there are all sorts of times when you or your partner will not achieve orgasm or get an erection, or you'll come too quickly, slowly, or not at all. Common reasons include tiredness, stress, anxiety, depression, physical illness, drugs, alcohol, effects of aging, or ongoing tension in your relationship. And sometimes it occurs for no good reason—"just because."

Here's a common story: "The main point of sex is to reach orgasm, and it's not good sex unless that happens!" Now if you cling tightly to this story, what do you think happens? This creates an intense atmosphere where there's real pressure to perform and achieve your goal. This in turn commonly leads to "performance anxiety": a feeling of stress or pressure or fear of failure when you come to have sex. And the problem is your sexual organs "switch off" when you're stressed or anxious, making it almost impossible to reach orgasm, control ejaculation, or keep an erection. So the more pressure you feel to "perform," the more likely you are to have sexual problems. Spot the vicious cycle, anyone? And if this cycle continues, before long, one or both partners start avoiding sex altogether because it becomes so fraught with unpleasant feelings!

If you make your sex life values-focused rather than goal-focused, then you can readily break this vicious cycle. Instead of focusing on erections and orgasms, you can use sex as a way to connect with and care for your partner. With this attitude, you are free. Connection and caring can happen in many different ways, regardless of whether you get an erection or have an orgasm. You can enact these values through kissing, hugging, massage, oral sex, masturbation, having a bath together, or through snuggling up on the couch with all your clothes on! You could go to bed and explore each other's bodies without even trying to have intercourse. You could try touching each other in different ways to see what feels pleasurable. You could try exploring every part of the body, not just breasts or genitals. You could have intercourse without even attempting to achieve an orgasm: doing it purely and simply to share pleasure or create a sense of connection. Of course, your mind would probably complain, *That's not real sex!*—but what would it cost you to hold on tightly to that one?

One important thing to remember in all this: the value of caring is absolutely vital. Sex won't always go the way you'd prefer. That's a given. So when the undesirable happens, if you get lost inside-your-mind or flick into reactivity mode, then you may say or do all sorts of hurtful things that will shatter trust and intimacy. This in turn worsens your sex life in the long run. So the message is simple: tune into your values around caring and, regardless of what happens, make sex safe!

sex and engaging

Mindfulness can wonderfully enhance physical intimacy. Whether you're kissing, hugging, caressing, nuzzling, holding hands, stroking, undressing, embracing, or having foreplay, oral sex, or intercourse, mindfulness can intensify both the pleasure and the sense of deep connection. When you tune into the sensations in your own body and tune into the reactions of your partner, sex becomes an absorbing and engaging experience—far more pleasurable than when you're all caught up in your thoughts or focused on achieving the goal of orgasm.

plenty of options

If we define "intimacy" broadly to include all three components—physical, emotional, and psychological—then clearly there are many ways of building it. Here are just a few to get you started: talking about your feelings, sharing your hopes and dreams, cuddling, discussing your philosophy of life, holding hands, revealing your deepest fears, kissing passionately, having a bath together, sharing fond memories, having intercourse, planning a holiday. Provided both partners are open, engaged, and caring, the opportunities for intimacy are endless; all you need is to use your imagination.

CHAPTER 22

old word, new take

We all get hurt in life. Sometimes others hurt us intentionally: perhaps out of racism, prejudice, competitiveness, or revenge. Or perhaps out of anger, or cruelty, or the desire to impress others. Far more often, others hurt us unintentionally: out of anxiety, insecurity, envy, jealousy, or sheer ignorance.

Ignorance is a big factor in hurting others. Think about how often you have unintentionally hurt someone you truly care about by saying or doing something that you never expected to be hurtful. Lack of awareness is another common culprit. How often have you upset or hurt someone simply because you did not pay attention to what you were doing and how it was affecting them? Or because you were so caught up in your own thoughts and feelings and struggles that you were unaware of theirs?

Regardless of the motivation, whenever somebody hurts us, we feel pain. And once it has happened, it has happened. We can't go back in time and alter it. At times, we are able to accept the hurt and move on with our lives. However, all too often, we hold on to it and magnify it. For example, we may get angry about what happened and take it out on the people around us, often hurting others in the process. Or we may replay those painful memories over and over, hurting ourselves repeatedly to no avail. We may hatch revenge fantasies, which magnify our anger and resentment, leading to more dissatisfaction. Or we may drink, smoke, eat food, take drugs, or otherwise try to distract ourselves from the pain.

Our mind says things like these: *Why me? How could this happen? This isn't fair! I don't deserve this.* If the nature of the hurt was major, your mind may even claim that you'll never get over it; that you are irreparably damaged by what has happened, or perhaps that you even deserved it! One thing's for sure: if you get absorbed in these stories, they rapidly suck you dry of health and vitality.

Naturally when something reminds you of pain from your past, painful thoughts and feelings are likely to show up. You can't stop that from happening. That's the way your brain is hardwired. But if you clutch those thoughts and feelings and refuse to let go, you turn them into a mass of seething resentment. This does not allow healing; instead it opens your wounds and pours in salt. The word "resentment" comes from the French *resentir*, which means "to feel again." When you hold on to resentment, you will relive the pain, again and again and again.

In Buddhism, there's a saying: resentment is like holding a red hot coal in order to throw it at someone else. When you hold on to hurts from the past, you cultivate feelings of anger, resentment, and revenge. These feelings hurt you, not the person who wronged you. It's like cutting yourself with a knife and hoping that the other person bleeds.

the antidote to resentment

So what is the antidote to resentment? You may not like the answer. It is forgiveness. But ACT has a new take on that old word—or rather an old take. You see, "forgiveness" is derived from the words "give" and "before." So you can think of forgiveness as "giving yourself back what was there before." In other words, "bad stuff" happens, and what you're left with is anger and resentment. But what did you have *before* the "bad stuff" happened? You had peace of mind and contentment; you were able to live in the present rather than miserably dwelling on the past. So "forgiveness" means you give this back to yourself. It is not something you do for anyone else; it is something you do purely for your own benefit.

Here's how ACT sees forgiveness:

- It is to relieve your own suffering—to let you get on with your life.

- It doesn't mean forgetting, excusing, pardoning, trivializing, or justifying any of the bad stuff that happened.

- It doesn't mean you have to say or do anything to the other(s) involved.

- It is something you do purely for yourself. You give yourself back what was there before—your life, your well-being, and your vitality!

What Does Forgiveness Require?

Forgiveness requires LOVE. When painful thoughts and memories show up, practice letting go. Notice they are present—name them if you like—and let them come and go like leaves on a stream. Or squash them in your fist, then open up your hand and say, "Letting go." Or simply engage in whatever you are doing in this moment: notice what you can see, hear, touch, taste, and smell. As you bring up the lights on the whole stage show, these thoughts and memories become only one small part of the whole spectacle.

When a painful feeling such as anger or resentment appears, remember to NAME it and tame it: notice the feeling, acknowledge it, make room for it, and expand awareness. Let the feeling come and go in its own good time without acting on it, struggling with it, or dwelling on it.

Again and again, come back to the basic principles of psychological flexibility: get present, open up, and do what matters—that is, act on your values. Make this a conscious choice instead of mindlessly indulging in self-defeating behaviors such as lashing out, brooding on the unchangeable past, or trying to get rid of your pain through food, drink, drugs, TV, and so on. Of course this is simple advice to give, but it's not easy to do. For most of us, it just doesn't come naturally. Still, if you truly value health, vitality, peace of mind, living in the present, and getting on with your life, then isn't it worth the effort?

if your partner is willing

Many couples find it is very healing to create their own forgiveness ritual. Following are the basic elements. You can use your own creativity to adapt this into something more personal.

Step 1: Each partner writes a letter that completes these three sentences:

■ The thoughts, feelings, and memories I've been holding on to are:

■ Holding on to all this has hurt our relationship in the following ways:

■ I want to build a better relationship, based on the following values:

Step 2: At the end of the letter, each partner writes in his or her own words some sort of commitment to let all these painful thoughts and feelings come and go without holding on.

Step 3: Choose a special place and read your letters aloud to each other. This could be anywhere from a special room in your house, to a park or a beach. As one partner reads, the other listens mindfully and compassionately.

Step 4: Do something that symbolizes starting over—for example, burn the letters and scatter the ashes.

Step 5: Do something to connect lovingly—for example, kiss, hug, go out to dinner, or have a bath together.

Where Does Trust Come In?

Forgiveness does not equate to trust. If your partner has deceived, betrayed, or misled you, then trust can take a long time to rebuild. So now it's time to look at ...

CHAPTER 23

building a trust fund

"How could he do that to me?"

"Why did I believe her?"

"Why didn't I see it coming?"

"How can I ever trust him again?"

When someone you love deceives or betrays you, it hurts. And those wounds may take a long time to heal. If your partner has cheated, lied, deceived, betrayed, manipulated, or harmed you, then you will need to make a choice about whether or not to continue your relationship. This is never easy, and your choice will depend on many factors, including children, finances, mitigating circumstances, the nature of the betrayal, and how often it has happened in the past. So make sure to practice plenty of self-compassion while you take the time necessary to make this difficult decision. Acknowledge your pain and stress—and be kind to yourself.

blind trust vs. mindful trust

If you do choose to stay, you will have some hard work ahead of you. If you've been hurt, abused, or deceived by a person you trust deeply, it usually takes a long time before you feel safe and secure with her again. So if you do choose to stay, you can expect to have plenty of thoughts and feelings of suspicion, insecurity, doubt, jealousy, or anxiety. And if you want your relationship to survive, recover, and thrive, then are you willing to open up and make room for these feelings while doing the hard work of rebuilding trust? If your answer is no, then you are stuck, and you will remain stuck until you either leave the relationship or commit to working on it. In that case, you will need plenty of self-compassion.

However, if your answer is yes, that you are willing to do the hard work of rebuilding, then it's important to distinguish between blind trust and mindful trust. "Blind trust" means you trust someone without bothering to assess whether he deserves it. "Mindful trust" means you see this person with your eyes open: you assess what she says and does, and trust her only if she earns it. So as you rebuild your relationship, you'll want to pay attention to these questions:

- Is your partner being honest, open, and truthful, or does he tend to lie, hide, and deceive?

- Is she sincere? Does she truly mean what she says?

- Is he reliable? Does he follow through on his promises?

- Is she responsible? Does she consider the consequences of her actions?

- Is he competent? Is he capable of actually doing what he promises?

If your partner acts sincerely, reliably, responsibly, and competently, *and* if you can directly observe this as opposed to taking her word for it, *and* if she maintains this over the long haul, then *over time*, you may gradually reestablish trust.

Keep in mind that you can't control the feelings of trust; you can only control the actions. So if you want to trust your partner again, then begin with small actions: trust him in tiny little ways and see if he proves worthy. In other words, assess his words and actions. If your partner proves "trustworthy," you can then, over time, take larger actions of trust while curiously observing the consequences. Step by step, you can keep on doing this, all the while making room for those perfectly normal feelings of anxiety, insecurity, and doubt. And if your partner continues to respond appropriately, then maybe, after a while, you will start once more to experience the feeling of trust. Of course, it's not a feeling in the same sense as emotions such as fear, anger, and sadness. It is more a sense of security, comfort, or safety.

Naturally you will have to find a healthy balance between actions of self-protection and actions of trust. In other words, if your husband has cheated on you, it's reasonable to call him at the office when he says he's working late. If your wife has frittered the mortgage away on gambling, it's reasonable to keep an eye on all her bank accounts. As genuine trust is gradually reestablished, these self-protective actions will become less necessary. The key is to find a healthy balance—one that's workable. If it's all about self-protection, you'll never repair the relationship; but if it's all about trust and you neglect your self-protection, then you're taking foolish risks. So find a balance that works and expect that balance to shift over time (assuming your partner continues to prove trustworthy). And be realistic about time frames; depending on what he did, this may take many months or even years.

Finally, acknowledge that you can never have certainty. If you want absolute certainty that your partner will never again betray you, the only way you can achieve that is to end the relationship. So if you choose to stay, are you willing to make room for uncertainty? To loosen your grip on "I'll get hurt again," breathe into that knot inside your stomach and make some space for that tightness in your chest.

if you've betrayed your partner's trust

I've written this chapter as if you are the one who was betrayed, but it could well be the other way around. Or perhaps you both betrayed each other. If you *have* betrayed your partner's trust, you'll probably have to work very hard to regain it. It's likely you will have to prove yourself to be reliable, competent, responsible, and sincere—and not just prove it once or twice, but over and over again. And you will need to make room for your partner's suspicion and reluctance to trust you again. You'll also need to let go of stories like "She should have gotten over it by now" or "Why is he taking so long to trust me again?" It may take weeks, months, or years before you rebuild the trust fund. So are you willing to cultivate patience and to make room for your own frustration and impatience?

At times, when you see your partner's pain, you may feel anxious, sad, or guilty. Are you willing to make room for those feelings? Are you willing to breathe into them, open up around them, and continue to engage fully with your partner—to stay with her rather than avoiding her? This is important. If you're not willing to accept those feelings, you will inevitably end up acting in self-defeating ways. For example, you may try to push them away by becoming angry. Anger feels empowering but does not bode well for healing and repairing. Or you may try to suppress your feelings with drugs, food, cigarettes, or alcohol. This is obviously not good for your own health and well-being. Or you may try to distract yourself by getting very busy, watching TV, or surfing the Net; this wastes a lot of time and does nothing constructive to repair your relationship. You may even try to avoid your partner because you don't like how you feel when you see his pain, but such avoidance would spell disaster in terms of rebuilding.

So instead of running from these feelings, use them to connect with your values: What do your feelings tell you about what matters to you? How can you act on those values?

Also use these feelings to cultivate compassion for both yourself and your partner. Yes, you deserve compassion too! Beating yourself up will not alter the past or compensate for what happened. The more you practice self-compassion, the easier you'll find it to be compassionate for your partner, which is what she needs from you.

a few words on temptation

At times, we all feel tempted to do things that would be destructive to our relationship: to lie, deceive, manipulate, or hurt our partner. From an ACT perspective, there is nothing "wrong" or "abnormal" about this; these are normal thoughts, feelings, and urges, and they are extremely common. The question is always one of workability. In the short run, if you act on these thoughts and feelings, they might well give you pleasure or satisfaction—but in the long run, will they deepen and strengthen your relationship?

While you can't stop yourself from feeling tempted, you can choose how you respond to those feelings. For example, you might feel like having sex with someone else, but you don't have to do it! You can bring mindfulness to your thoughts and feelings, flip from automatic pilot to awareness mode, and consciously take control of your arms and legs. You can then tune into your values around trust, respect, care, fairness, and integrity, and base your actions on your values rather than your urges. In doing this consistently, you reap a double reward. Not only do you show your partner he can trust you, you also build trust in yourself. This is a great gift. Life will test you in a million different ways. When you can trust yourself to respond wisely, then you know you have a great ally by your side.

CHAPTER 24

let your self go

In my childhood days, we used to play a game called "king of the castle." Two kids would race each other up a hill or a slope, or clamber up on top of a high wall, and whoever reached the top first would shout down at the other, "I'm the king of the castle, and you're the dirty rascal!" The "king" feels wonderful: he is on top of the world, triumphant, looking down and laughing at the "dirty rascal" below. But the "dirty rascal" does not feel good at all. Alas, all too often adult couples play a very similar game.

comparing yourself with your partner

Does your mind ever compare you with your partner? Does it claim that you are superior, smarter, or stronger? Does it sometimes suggest that perhaps you deserve someone better? Or does it tell you that you are inferior, lesser, dumber, and weaker than your partner? Or does it perhaps alternate? Stories about ourselves are very enticing; they easily draw us in and keep us absorbed. If you get caught up in "I'm superior," you are likely to look down on your partner, dismiss his ideas, discount his needs, or lack respect for him. If you get caught up in "I'm inferior," you are likely to become insecure, anxious, fearful of rejection, needy for reassurance, demanding of approval, or neglectful of your own needs. So holding on tightly to these stories is not useful.

Your mind may not go along with this. It may protest, *But it's true!* And let's face it, if your mind wants to "prove" you're superior, it can find plenty of ways in which you surpass your partner. And if your mind wants to "prove" you're inferior, it can find all sorts of things your partner does better than you. This is always possible because if you put any two humans together, they will inevitably have different "strengths" and "weaknesses." So to feel superior, simply focus on all the ways in which you are "stronger." And to feel inferior, simply focus on all the ways in which you are "weaker." I guarantee you, if you look hard enough, there will be no shortage of either. (By the way, you'll notice I've put "weaker" and "stronger" in quotes; this is to remind you that these are *judgments*, not *facts*. What one person judges a weakness, another may see as a strength. For example, I judge it a strength that I am able to cry freely when I am sad; yet some people might judge this a weakness, especially if they are fused with "Men shouldn't cry!")

Given how easily you can "prove" your self-assessment, why waste your time trying to dispute it? Rather than debate whether it's "true or false," consider it in terms of workability. Ask yourself honestly, does holding on tightly to your self-description work to make your relationship rich and rewarding? Clutching "I'm superior" may make you feel better about yourself, but it commonly leads to arrogance, selfishness, or egotism, and the neglect of values around equality and fairness. Clinging to "I'm inferior" commonly leads to insecurity, jealousy, depression, anxiety, or neediness, and the neglect of values around self-care and self-respect. Thus neither story is helpful to your relationship.

Hopefully you can see that we all benefit from holding our self-descriptions, positive or negative, lightly. If your mind tells you a positive self-description, you can smile and say, "Hmmm. Interesting story." If your mind tells you a negative self-description, you can smile and say, "Hmmm. Interesting story." If your mind compares you with your partner, you can smile and name it: "Aha! Comparing again!"

Like any other thoughts, you can let your self-descriptions come and go; you can let them go past like passing cars or float on by like leaves upon a stream. And instead of getting absorbed in these self-descriptions, you can tune into your values: What sort of partner do you want to be? What do you want to stand for? Do you have values around equality, fairness, respect, and caring? What would happen if you let those values guide your actions rather than being ruled by your self-description?

changing behavior: easier said than done?

It's never easy to make changes in long-term patterns of behavior. Your mind has been telling you you're superior or inferior (or both) for many, many years, and you have a well-developed habit of picking those stories up and becoming very absorbed in them. So if you're finding it hard to put them down, I suggest that you practice the Leaves on a Stream Exercise (see chapter 10) and/or the Mindful Breathing Exercise (see chapter 11) for at least five to ten minutes once or twice a day (more is better!). As you repeatedly enter the "mental space" of mindfulness, you are likely to discover something very empowering: a higher sense of self that is beyond any words. In ACT, we call this part of you "the observing self."

We can talk about "self" in many different ways, but in the Western world, we commonly limit ourselves to two ways: (1) the physical self—our body and (2) the thinking self—our mind. However, there is a third aspect of self, as I mentioned before, that we use whenever we practice mindfulness. When you observe your thoughts, who is observing them? When you notice that voice chattering away inside your head, who is noticing it? When you observe your breath, who is observing? When you notice your feelings, who is noticing them? In ACT, we generally call this part of you the *observing self*. It is a part of every human being that is largely overlooked by Western culture.

In common everyday language, we use the word "mind" without recognizing that it has two major elements to it: the thinking self and the observing self. We are all very familiar with the thinking self; it is that part of us that throws up a never-ending stream of words and pictures: thoughts, beliefs, memories, fantasies, plans, daydreams, opinions, judgments, and so on. So when we use the word "mind," we are generally referring to the thinking self. In contrast, many people have no concept of the observing self: that part of you which silently notices or observes. We don't even have a word for it in everyday language; the closest terms we have are "awareness" or "consciousness."

The thinking self and the physical self (your body) work in unison to create the stage show of life. The physical self interacts with the world through all the five senses, and in doing so it produces all your sensations: everything that you can see, hear, touch, taste, and smell. The thinking self produces all your thoughts, memories, and images. Your feelings and emotions are a mixture of sensations, images, memories, and thoughts. So the thinking self and the physical self work together to put on the stage show of life: a spectacle that consists of all your thoughts, all your feelings, and everything you can see, hear, touch, taste, and smell. And that show continually changes. The observing self is the part of you that can watch the show: it can focus in on any part of it, or step back and take it all in at once. And although the show keeps changing, the observing self does not. Every single mindfulness exercise you do involves this part of you. When you watch your thoughts, when you observe your breath, when you notice and make room for your feelings, when you are opening up, letting go, or engaging, this is your observing self at work. (If you want to know more about the observing self, you may like to read my first book, *The Happiness Trap*. See Recommended Reading.).

Your observing self is a powerful ally when it comes to loosening your grip on your self-description. It helps you to see that your self-description is nothing more than a collection of thoughts. And regardless of how true or false they may be, they are only one small element of the amazing stage show of life. When you step back from the stage and watch the show, this becomes clear. You recognize thoughts for what they are: nothing more than words or pictures or sounds. Whether they are true or false is beside the point; the point is, if you grip them too tightly, you'll have problems. In the "mental space" of the observing self, your self-description loses its hold on you. The farther you step back from the stage, the more you see this story for what it is: just a performer trying to capture your attention; desperate to steal the show, it tries to step into the spotlight and plunge the rest of the stage into darkness. And sometimes it succeeds. But as you develop your mindfulness skills, you will be able to bring up the lights on the entire stage rather than allowing any one performer to dominate.

In the short run, letting go of these self-descriptions may be uncomfortable. For example, if you rely on the "superior" story for a sense of self-worth, you may discover that as you let go of it, anxiety, insecurity, or self-doubt may show up. Similarly if you let go of your "inferior" story and start acting on your values around self-respect and self-care, then you may well experience fear of rejection or getting hurt. So ask yourself: "Am I willing to make room for discomfort in order to build a better, richer, relationship?" If yes, then practice LOVE—letting go, opening up, acting on values, engaging. If no, then accept that you're stuck—and practice self-compassion until you get moving again.

CHAPTER 25

and now, time for some fun!

One important value that we've ignored so far is having fun. If you neglect this value, a relationship tends to become very heavy and serious. As the proverb goes, "All work and no play make Jack a dull boy."

creating connection rituals

Alas, in our busy, stressful lives, we can easily forget to make time for fun and games. So it's very useful to set up some regular "connection rituals." A *connection ritual* is any activity that you do on a regular basis where the main purpose is to strengthen your bond with your partner. You can use these rituals to have fun, play games, share pleasure, support each other, express affection, or deepen intimacy. Simple connection rituals include:

- Talking about your day when you get home from work

- Having a heart-to-heart over a drink

- Going on a date: dinner, movies, bowling, dancing, and so on

- Sharing physical activities, such as running, swimming, walking, or yoga

- Sharing spiritual activities, such as meditation or going to church

- Sharing hobbies, crafts, or creative activities

- Playing games

- Going on family outings

- Having friends over for dinner

- Physical intimacy, ranging from cuddling on the couch to having sex

Making time to connect is vital for a healthy long-term relationship. So use this list to get you thinking, then pull out your journal or worksheet and jot down some ideas for your own rituals.

if your partner is willing

Jointly brainstorm ways in which you can connect more regularly. You can use the previous suggestions as a guide. Also think back on ways you connected in the past. Once you've generated a list of ideas, pick the most workable options and then decide when and where you will actually do them.

Many couples find it helpful to schedule a "date night." Once a week, you—just the two of you—go on a date. You don't socialize with friends on these dates; you just appreciate being with each other. If this appeals to you, then pull out your calendar and write the dates in, at least a month ahead. If you don't do this, then as you get caught up in the demands of daily life, your dates will be forgotten. (And if once a week is not possible, then adapt this idea to suit your own circumstances.)

One simple ritual that many couples find helpful is to have a regular heart-to-heart talk about their relationship: a "check-in" to see how, from both points of view, the relationship is going. This could be something you do over dinner or a drink, or during a walk in the park, or even as part of your date night. Some couples do this every couple of weeks; others find once a month works better. You could try it out and adapt it to suit your needs. Here are some questions that you might find useful during these talks:

- What's working in our relationship? What have you noticed that you approve of?

- What have you appreciated most in the last two weeks?

- When have you felt most connected, satisfied, loved, supported, understood, accepted, or cared for?

- What's not working? And what could we do differently that might work better?

When you plan dates or other connection rituals, think about ways to bring fun, games, leisure, and pleasure into your relationship. Taking turns, ask and answer these questions:

- What is your idea of fun?

- What have we done in the past that was fun?

- What makes you laugh and smile?

- When do you feel most alive?

- What fills you with joy?

- What do we do currently that is fun for you?

- How could we have more fun in the future?

Once you've answered these questions, convert them into plans. Schedule some activities that you can do on a regular basis simply to have fun or pleasure together. (And make sure when you do them, you engage fully; you certainly won't have much fun if you're inside-your-mind!)

keep looking into your heart

ACT advocates that you reflect on your values regularly: think about them, talk about them, write about them, or even meditate on them. This helps you to keep the "big picture" in mind: to stay in touch with what matters in the long run. When you're bogged down in unhelpful stories; hurting from fights and squabbles; disappointed or irritated by your partner's differences; feeling bored, trapped, disillusioned, cheated, or dissatisfied, then you can always turn to your values for a helping hand: to pull you up and help you get back on track.

Your values, however, won't stack up neatly like books in a bookcase. They may well pull you in different directions, so you will often need to choose between them. And in different situations, some values will take priority over others. Psychologist John Forsyth uses the analogy of a cube. If you hold a cube in your hands and turn it around, in some positions you see only one side of it; in other positions you may see two or three sides. But three is the maximum. So no matter how you hold it, there will always be at least three sides that you *can't* see. Those sides have not ceased to exist; they are merely out of sight temporarily. Turn the cube over, and they instantly come back into view. Similarly, in any given moment, some values come to the forefront and others fall back.

Thus one important aspect of psychological flexibility is the ability to shift between values as required. To do this, you'll need to hold them lightly. Yes, values—just like any other thoughts—will create problems if you grasp them tightly; they will turn into rules and become rigid, restrictive, or oppressive. So come back to the notion of values as a compass. You want to pull your compass out from time to time, check that you're headed in the right direction, and then put it away in your backpack until you need it again. You won't enjoy your journey if you are clutching the compass tightly each step of the way.

Values are so useful. Wherever you go, they are with you. You can use them to guide and inspire you in any moment. You can use them as a reminder or a wake-up call to pull you out of the smog and into the valley. So before you read on to the end, I recommend you revisit chapter 7 and once again take a good, long look into your heart. This will equip you well as ...

CHAPTER 26

the adventure continues

Mark Twain once wrote, "To cease smoking is the easiest thing I ever did. I ought to know because I've done it a thousand times." Even if we've never smoked, most of us can relate to this witty observation. How often have you said, "I'm never going to do that again!" and, sure enough, half an hour later you go and do it? How often have you thought, *Next time, I'm going to handle this differently!* And next time comes around and to your shock and horror, you end up doing the same old thing! The fact is, deeply entrenched behaviors are not that easy to stop. If you doubt this, take a good look at yourself: have you successfully eliminated all your "bad habits"? (If so, congratulations: you are the first perfect human being in the history of the world and you should definitely write a book about it!)

realism and relapse

By the time your relationship is in trouble, both you and your partner will have established a large number of self-defeating habits. And some of these have been present since you were a child, such as your tendency to fuse with judgments, rules, and expectations. Awareness of these habits is not enough. Only repeated practice of LOVE will reverse the DRAIN.

Having said that, let's be realistic. Whoever said "Practice makes perfect" was clearly deluded. There's no such thing as perfection. Practice will help you establish better relationship skills, but it will not permanently eliminate all your self-defeating behaviors. You and your partner will screw up, make mistakes, and fall back into "bad habits." This will happen again and again and again.

But that doesn't mean you should "give up." It just means "be realistic." With practice, you can become much better at living by your values as well as dispersing your smog, engaging with your partner, fighting fairly, making repair attempts, practicing forgiveness and compassion, asking nicely, expressing appreciation, and accepting your differences. So the more you practice, the better the outlook for the future. At the same time, let go of unrealistic expectations. Neither you nor your partner will always do what's workable. And no matter how much you apply the principles of LOVE, and no matter how "second nature" they become, there will always be times when you forget and fall back into old ways.

That's why, when I counsel couples, I always discuss the inevitability of "relapse." I might say, "Okay, so she's just made a commitment that from now on, instead of yelling at you and criticizing you, she'll explain calmly and respectfully why she's annoyed. Now I'm sure she's sincere; she seems genuinely determined to work on this. My question is, how likely is it that she will never, ever yell at you or criticize you again?" In saying this, I'm not aiming to undermine the commitment; I am simply aiming to introduce some realism.

Most couples appreciate this. It helps them to loosen their grip on the "perfect partner" story. If one partner protests, "No, that's not good enough. I need to know that it will never happen again," then we return to workability. How does it work, holding tightly to the expectation that your partner will change overnight and never relapse? Does it help you cultivate acceptance and understanding? Or does it simply create more tension and conflict?

Obviously there may be some types of behavior where relapse is not acceptable. If your partner has been having sex with other people, physically abusing you, or stealing your money and gambling with it, then you may well choose to leave him rather than run the risk of it happening again. Indeed many people will probably advise you to do this. However, ultimately it's your decision, not anyone else's. So if you do choose to stay with your partner, knowing he has a track record of such behaviors, then be realistic; recognize that relapse is a genuine possibility, no matter how much he swears it won't happen. (And revisit chapter 23 on building trust.)

screwing up

Because human beings screw up so often, I repeatedly ask my clients these three questions:

- When your partner screws up, how would you ideally respond?

- When you screw up, how would you ideally like your partner to respond?

- When either one of you screws up, what would you ideally say or do to handle it effectively and make amends?

Before answering these questions, get in touch with your values; reflect on the sort of partner you want to be. Think again of "door mats" and "battering rams," "sharks" and "puppy dogs." These playful terms refer to self-defeating habits: patterns of behavior you tend to do mindlessly, on automatic pilot. If you could respond mindfully, acting on your deepest values, then what would you say and do when one of you screws up? Are you willing to forgive, let go, and move on? Are you willing to make room for your painful feelings, let go of unhelpful thoughts, and discuss the issue in a way that allows for repairs? Are you willing to apply the principles of positive reinforcement, as described in chapter 18, to catch your partner doing it right and thank her rather than come down hard when she does it wrong? And if not, what will your lack of willingness cost you in the long run?

Please take some time to ponder the three questions at the beginning of this section, and write your answers down in your journal or worksheet. And if your partner is willing, then both of you do the exercise and discuss your answers.

tying it all together

One reading of this book will not be enough for it all to sink in. It is intended as a reference book: a resource you can return to again and again to revisit ideas, repeat exercises, and refresh your memory. My hope is that you can open it up at random and always find something that's personally relevant and useful. A few useful things to remember include these:

- Love and pain are dance partners; they go hand in hand.

- You can't always get what you want.

- There's no such thing as the perfect partner.

- Complex issues rarely have simple answers.

- You can't control your partner, but you can control yourself!

- You *can* influence your partner, but the carrot is far more workable than the stick.

- Conflict is inevitable. But fair fighting, making repairs, and practicing compassion will make it much less destructive.

- Feelings of love come and go; actions of love can be taken in any moment.

We could easily expand this list to several pages, but the essence of the book—to repair and deepen your relationship—can be summarized in two main ideas:

1. Reduce the DRAIN: disconnection, reactivity, avoidance, dwelling inside-your-mind, and neglecting your values.

2. Increase the LOVE: letting go, opening up, valuing, and engaging.

In terms of valuing, we've mainly focused on caring, connection, and contribution. There are obviously many other values we could have mentioned, but these three are particularly important. Trying to build a rich relationship without them is like trying to build a castle on a swamp.

We've also considered the importance of working on yourself and turning yourself into the best partner you can be. Very often, when one partner starts acting mindfully, there's a rapid drop in tension and conflict within the relationship. And the more you act on your values around care, kindness, nurturing, forgiveness, acceptance, compassion, assertiveness, equality, and respect, the more likely your partner is to respond positively.

Naturally this is easier said than done. There will always be plenty of barriers in your way. To quote Father Alfred D'Souza: "For a long time it has seemed to me that life was about to begin—real life. But there was always some obstacle in the way, something to be got through first, some unfinished business, time still to be served, a debt to be paid. Then life would begin. At last it dawned on me that these obstacles were my life."

An intimate relationship brings no shortage of obstacles: problems, difficulties, and issues come in all shapes and forms. But with the right attitude, these challenges can become a source of growth. They give you the opportunity to not only increase psychological flexibility, but also to strengthen and deepen the bonds between you. The attitude required is willingness. Willingness to learn, grow, and adapt. Willingness to embrace reality, even when it fails to meet your expectations. Willingness to approach your differences and find constructive, caring ways of resolving or accepting them. Willingness to be flexible and adaptable in dealing with the ever-changing circumstances of life. Willingness to connect with, care for, and contribute to your partner— even when the going gets tough and tedious. Willingness to let go, open up, value, and engage—again and again and again, without giving up.

parting words

The principles of LOVE are simple, but they are not easy. They require hard work, practice, and dedication. The great poet Rainer Maria Rilke put it this way: "For one human being to love another: that is perhaps the most difficult of our tasks; the ultimate, the last test and proof, the work for which all other work is but preparation." Fortunately, although the work is hard, it gives huge rewards.

Love is a great adventure. It brings wonder and fear, pleasure and pain, hardship and joy. The trick is to embrace every part of it. The wonder and joy energize you; the pain softens you up and opens your heart. So appreciate the adventure while it lasts. Make the most of it. Learn from it. Grow from it. When the going gets tough—and it will— then treat yourself kindly. And regardless of how you are feeling, *ACT WITH LOVE.*

appendix:
when it's over, it's over

This is the one part of this book I didn't want to write. My hope was that by applying LOVE—letting go, opening up, valuing, and engaging— you would resolve your issues, reconcile your differences, and deepen and strengthen your relationship. Sadly sometimes it just doesn't work out that way. Sometimes you try everything humanly possible and you just can't seem to make it work. Obviously reading a book such as this does not exhaust the many possibilities for help. There are other books I've listed in the resources section, all of which can be very useful. Also, many couples find a therapist or counselor of huge help, as well as individual therapy, or a combination of both.

If, however, you've reached that point of no return and you're certain that breaking up is the right choice for you, then aim to do so with LOVE. As you leave the relationship, tune into your values and be the person you want to be. An amicable separation or divorce is better for everyone involved, especially if children are involved. When former partners get bogged down in bitter lawsuits and hostile custody battles, the lawyers make a small fortune, but everyone else suffers miserably. And it's heartbreaking when parents use their children as weapons to hurt one another; the children always get hurt during the process.

So, if you choose to leave, then what do you want to stand for as you do so? Do you want to stand for revenge, bitterness, hostility? For dragging the kids through the courts? For hurting others, no matter what the cost? Or do you want to stand for something that you can be proud of when you look back on this difficult period of your life—such as openness, honesty, fairness, kindness, or taking care of the children's best interests?

Also consider this: what unhelpful stories can you let go of? Revenge stories are especially seductive: "She's hurt me, so I'll hurt her!" Your mind says that this will make you feel better, but this is highly unlikely. And even if revenge does give you some short-term satisfaction, later on you are likely to regret it. So why invest your time, money, and energy on a bitter, hostile, drawn-out, tempestuous breakup, when there is no long-term benefit for either of you?

Also keep in mind that every painful situation provides you with an opportunity to develop psychological flexibility, so find the gold in the garbage. After all, if you're going through hell, you might as well get some benefit from it. Ask yourself, how can I grow and develop from this? What might I learn about forgiveness, compassion, letting go, mindfulness, or acceptance? How might my own experience benefit others that I care about?

Return again and again to the principles of LOVE—letting go, opening up, valuing, and engaging. They are useful for every stage of a relationship: the beginning, the middle, and the end. And that goes for the most important relationship of all: the one you have with yourself. So tune into your values around kindness, caring, and compassion—and apply them to yourself. You will surely need them in the difficult times to follow.

resources

ACT workshops

I run a range of ACT workshops mainly for health professionals but also some for the general public. For details of Australian workshops, go to www.actmindfully.com.au. For details of workshops in the United States and other countries, go to www.thehappinesstrap.com.

CDs and worksheets

I have designed and recorded CDs such as *Mindfulness Skills*, volume 1, to help you develop and improve your mindfulness skills. You can order these, or download MP3 recordings, from the resources section on www.act-with-love.com. From the same site, you can also download a series of free worksheets to use in conjunction with the exercises in this book. When you visit www.act-with-love you'll discover it is nested within a larger website: www.thehappinesstrap.com. The larger website supports my first ACT-based book, *The Happiness Trap*; it contains many useful free ACT resources.

find an ACT therapist

To find an ACT therapist or to learn more about ACT, visit the official ACT website, www.contextualpsychology.org.

recommended reading

Comfort, Alex. 1991 *The New Joy of Sex.* New York: Crown Publishers.

Gottman, John, and Nan Silver. 1999. *The Seven Principles of Making Marriage Work.* New York: Three Rivers Press.

Harris, Russ. 2008. *The Happiness Trap: How to Stop Struggling and Start Living.* Boston: Trumpeter Books.

McKay, Matthew, Patrick Fanning, and Kim Paleg. 2006. *Couple Skills.* Oakland, CA: New Harbinger Publications.

Walser, Robyn D., and Darrah Westrup. 2009. *The Mindful Couple: Using Acceptance and Mindfulness to Enhance Vitality, Compassion, and Love.* Oakland, CA: New Harbinger Publications.

references

Gottman, John, and Nan Silver. 1999. *The Seven Principles of Making Marriage Work*. New York: Three Rivers Press.

Hayes, Steven C., Kirk Strosahl, and Kelly G. Wilson. 1999. *Acceptance and Commitment Therapy: An Experiential Approach to Behavior Change*. New York: Guilford.

Hayes, Steven C., Kelly G. Wilson, E. V. Gifford, Victoria Follette, and Kirk Strosahl. 1996. Experiential avoidance and behavioral disorders: A functional dimensional approach to diagnosis and treatment. *Journal of Consulting and Clinical Psychology*, 64(6): 1152–68.

Hite, Shere. 1976. *The Hite Report: A Nationwide Study of Female Sexuality*. New York: Seven Stories Press.

Neff, K. D. 2003. Self-compassion: An alternative conceptualization of a healthy attitude toward oneself. *Self and Identity*, 2, 85-102.

Nhat Hanh, Thic. 1976. *The Miracle of Mindfulness!* Boston: Beacon Press.

Weintraub, Stanley. 2001. *Silent Night: The Story of the World War I Christmas Truce*. New York: The Free Press.

Russ Harris, MD, is an acceptance and commitment therapy (ACT) trainer and author of *The Happiness Trap*. He lives in Perth, Australia, and travels around the world training psychologists and other health professionals in ACT. Visit him online at www.actmindfully.com.